Cuban FLAVOR

 Exploring the Island's Unique Places, People, and Cuisine

Writing & Photography By
LIZA GERSHMAN

Foreword By MARI AIXALÁ

Skyhorse Publishing

Also by Liza Gershman, with Skyhorse

Passage to China: A Photographic Celebration of the Silk Road

Drink Vermont: Beer, Wine, and Spirits of the Green Mountain State
With a foreword by Sam von Trapp

Skyhorse Publishing books may be purchased in bulk at special discounts for sales promotion, corporate gifts, fund-raising, or educational purposes. Special editions can also be created to specifications. For details, contact the Special Sales Department, Skyhorse Publishing, 307 West 36th Street, 11th Floor, New York, NY 10018 or info@ skyhorsepublishing.com.

Skyhorse® and Skyhorse Publishing® are registered trademarks of Skyhorse Publishing, Inc.®, a Delaware corporation.

Visit our website at www.skyhorsepublishing.com.

10 9 8 7 6 5 4 3 2

Library of Congress Cataloging-in-Publication Data is available on file.

Cover design by Jenny Zemanek
Cover photo credit Liza Gershman

Print ISBN: 978-1-5107-1012-2
Ebook ISBN: 978-1-5107-1014-6

Printed in China

For Shelby & Arthur, Betty & Marvin,
Nancy & Abby, Giedra, and Alastair

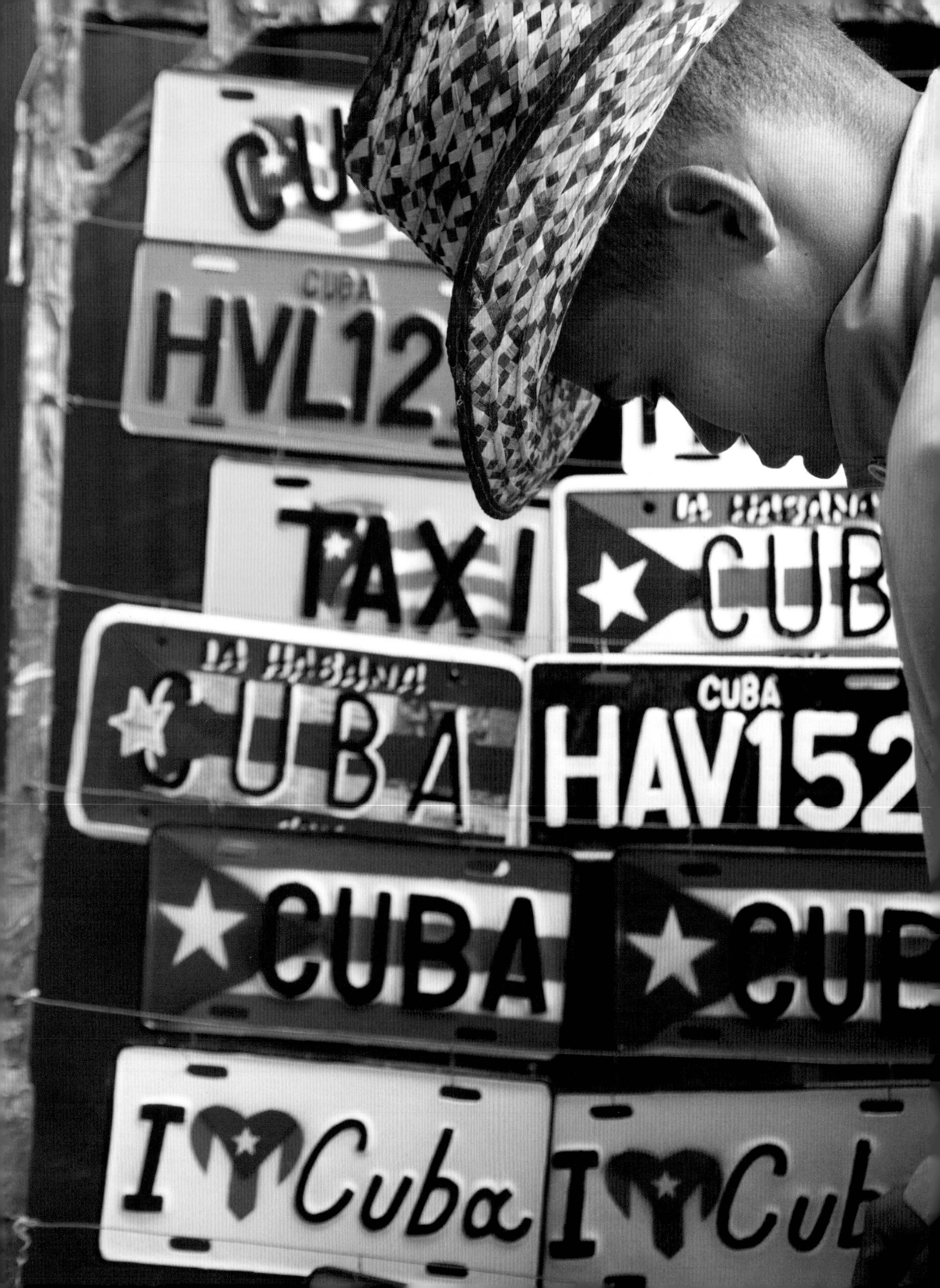
CUBA
HVL12
TAXI
CUBA
CUBA
HAV152
CUBA
I Cuba

table of contents

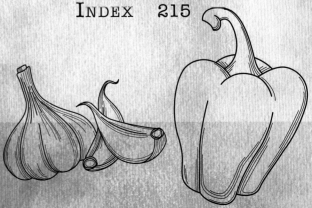

acknowledgments

They can print statistics and count the populations in hundreds of thousands, but to each man a city consists of no more than a few streets, a few houses, a few people. Remove those few and a city exists no longer except as a pain in the memory, like a pain of an amputated leg no longer there. —GRAHAM GREENE, **Our Man in Havana**

Thank you to my Cuban friends, hosts, and guides who have all welcomed me as family: Lancelot and Rayda Alonso, Yosniel, Alejandro, Junior, Mike, Carlos, Vivianne, Carey, Mariana, Claudia, Ray, Tony, and others.

Thank you to every friend who has schlepped through the streets of Havana, Trinidad, and Viñales with me in search of food, photos, and chefs! Debbie, Katie, Megan, Jessica, Lauren, Bonnie & Roger, Steve & Evie, Apple, Vik, Giedra, Darren, Andie, Ankur & Eileen, Christina & Tom, Asya, Annie, Raj & Shivani, and more!

Thank you to the US team for food and recipe assistance, props, and photo production. Fanny Pan, Leigh Noe, Courtney Atinsky, Sandbox Studios, and Laura Burch.

Thank you to Alastair Windeler for his constant support.

Thank you to Savannah Jones, for all of her incredible assistant work.

Thank you so much to the Forge household for their support: Gemma, Steve, Emily, Patrick, and Isabelle and Alfie.

Thank you to Rayne Wolf for friendship, encouragement, and editing.

Many thanks to Abigail and Kim, my wonderful editors, at Skyhorse for their help to make this passion project come to life.

And last but not least, to Carlos, my first Cuban friend, whom I have never found again.

Foreword

Ask a sixth-generation Cuban to write a succinct foreword for a Cuban cookbook? Did they ask the right bilingual, bicultural person? Clearly someone has not been briefed about my uprooted, exiled, immigrant life surrounded by enchanting storytellers with an incessant desire to recall what was great in Cuba *a la hora de comer* (when it was time to eat)?!

Nevertheless, I entertained the challenge. I began to take in and savor the fruits of Liza Gershman's labor and fell in love with a stunningly shot, spectacularly presented, elegant, sensual, and inspiring *libro de cocina* (cookbook). Much like all great recipes with fresh ingredients and *mucho amor* (much love), there's *nada mas* (no more) to be added. Liza serves up everything you could want on the pages and sections that follow.

Narrowing in on my succinct message, I'm taking a stab and issuing a warning: attention, all who dare open *Cuban Flavor*. Please be prepared to participate in a progressive journey through Cuba and its traditions that will delight your senses; engage your imagination; seduce you with their timeless, unparalleled magic; and maybe . . . just maybe . . . even stimulate your *apetito* (appetite). Just like a Cuban vintage Bacardi rum ad would read, Liza Gersham 's *Cuban Flavor* is "*sano, sabroso, y Cubano*" (healthy, tasty, and Cuban).

Eñjoy,
Mari Aixalá

*It was a city to visit, not a city to live in,
but it was the city where Wormold had first fallen
in love and he was held to it as though to the scene
of a disaster. Time gives poetry to a battlefield.*
—GRAHAM GREENE, OUR MAN IN HAVANA

introduction

My love affair with Cuba began long before my first visit in 2003, and my passion for Cuban food began long before then. I dreamed, like you may have too, of a rich blend of Native American, Taíno, Spanish, African, and Caribbean cuisines.

The story of Cuban cuisine is as diverse as its traditions and cultures. Colonized by the Spanish, and later the French, and built up by slaves from Africa and Haiti, as well as a population of Chinese immigrants, Cuba has a food culture with flavors that most closely resemble those found in Puerto Rico and the neighboring Dominican Republic. However, Cuba has a history and figurative spice all of its own. Cuban Flavor is not simply a beautiful cookbook, but rather an introduction to a revolutionary era of Cuban cuisine—truly a new frontier.

***

During the most difficult times in Cuba, known as the Special Period, opulent meals were served only to the elite connected to the government, while others sat by and starved. It was a time of great economic crisis in Cuba that began in 1989 with the dissolution of the Soviet Union (and their financial support of Cuba), and continued through the mid- to late-'90s. During this time, Cubans suffered greatly and endured shortages in fuel, food, and other resources. For many, a piece of bread with sugar was sustenance for the day.

Cuba's tropical climate has always been perfect for growing pineapple, guava, mango, and limes. The lapping sea delivers a bounty of crustaceans and fish. In a typical Cuban home kitchen, you'll find tools from the 1950s like pressure cookers and rice cookers, broken utensils, dull knives, and mismatched china. It's a wonder that anyone can actually cook. But the resilience of the Cuban people perfumes each savory dish, as always.

While rice and beans are staples of the Cuban diet, their cuisine is such a complex story—a tapestry of love and loss, woven so deeply into their culture going far beyond history or sustenance. To those of us more fortunate, Cuban cuisine can appear as a stroke of luck served up on a beautiful platter.

* * *

When I first visited Cuba in 2003, to my great disappointment, every meal was the same. We ate plain chicken, rice, and beans. Cuba was in a difficult financial period, and tourism had yet to really take hold. Since then, the cuisine has greatly transformed. A burgeoning connection to ingredients and spices inevitably brings European, Asian, and Latin flavors to the island, and chefs now have an opportunity to experiment with flavors through an increasingly hungry tourist population, with an insatiable appetite for more.

Traditional Cuban sauces nearly always contain oil, onions, red paprika, or aji cachucha, (the little sweet-spicy pepper found in local produce markets). However, even these simple items can be difficult to find because of chronic problems in food supply, and occasional acute food shortages. As a result, Cubans are deeply resourceful people, not only in the search for what is available on any given day, but also in their neighborly sharing economy, which plays itself out as a deep cultural understanding and celebration of what it is to live in the moment.

Meat, when available, is most often served stewed or slow cooked with garlic, onion, and simple spices. The island's signature dish, the delicious Ropa Vieja, or "rags," is shredded meat that has been simmered in a tomato-based criollo sauce. While the recipe traditionally calls for beef, Ropa Vieja has always been cooked in regular Cuban homes with pork, as it is often the available meat outside of restaurants.

For many years, the only available cooking oil was from pork fat, and this had to be sourced from private markets. Rare and precious, this pork fat was used for every meal and recycled as many times as possible. Most families subsisted on rice and one egg per person for the main meal of the day. If a family was lucky, then the one egg was fried with pork fat to add additional protein for nutrition.

The industry of raising swine has long been a great economic interest for Cuba. It began with the introduction of pigs to the island by the Spanish in the 1800s. Brought from ships to the area known as the Bay of Pigs, this farming practice thrived. During the Special Period, raising and breeding pigs in the bathtubs of Cuban homes was a very common practice, although illegal. Cubans broke the law out of sheer desperation for protein, and the meat from one "bathtub" pig could help to feed a Cuban family for almost a year. The risk was high, but the reward was more significant. These illegally raised bathtub pigs could also be sold by the families for profit in order to purchase other desperately needed essentials like rice, beans, plantains, vegetables, and the even more scarce cooking oil and tomato sauce.

Today, in every Cuban market one can find a traditional hanging piece of pork leg, as one does in the Spanish markets. But in Cuba, rather than a preserved delicacy, the leg is a piece of uncured meat that is used for ropa vieja, masa frita, and arroz moro (rice and black beans cooked together).

Paladares, or privately run restaurants, became legal in the 1990s. Often set up as home-based restaurants when they began out of private residences (once a simple affair with one, two, or three tables set in the owner's living room or anywhere else that they could fit), paladares enabled Cubans to earn money through private enterprise, which can be significantly greater than a salary from a government or state-run job. Now with the large demand from tourism and laws that passed in 2010, which allowed the paladares to run more like a modern restaurant rather than it resembling a meal cooked in a friend's grandmother's home, paladares have sprouted up around the country and are not just found in proprietors' homes, but also function as regular restaurants as well.

I always experience an internal conflict when visiting Cuba and eating at the paladares. While I know that my currency helps to support a handful of friends, I realize that the paradox exists in which others in Cuba cannot, and most likely will never be able to, share this experience or have access to such broad and plentiful food.

There is also a large influx of Italian cuisine in Havana, and you can see pizza and pasta on nearly every street corner. Additionally, a small Chinatown offers a variety of quasi-Eastern cuisine.

For the thriving paladares, food supply is also hard to come by, and items like lobster and spices must be purchased through a black market system. Some make purchases through the Cuban version of Craigslist, Revolico.com, while others barter with friends and suppliers they have come to know. But getting caught with something that is too "special," like dried cranberries on a salad (an item that has clearly been provided from someone coming from abroad), will raise eyebrows and put the chef in jeopardy. Every Cuban can tell you a daily tale of how they came to access the food in their kitchen. Imagine: a daily chore of searching for food, even if you had the financial wherewithal to purchase it.

Today, the food situation in Cuba is incredibly complex. Despite the increased access to food in this changing cultural and political landscape, most locals still rely on monthly food rations. Food excesses that we are so accustomed to in the developed world (including fine dining) continue to be a privilege of the new generation of elites—now the entrepreneurs of tourism—and of their clientele.

Stocking a Cuban home kitchen remains one of the biggest challenges of daily life as the average Cuban lives with a startling food scarcity that one can only describe as cruel. Havana, after all, is a city of two million people before tourists even touch the ground. While tourists dine at any of the estimated 1,700 paladares on the island, food prices for locals soar. Not only is there a dearth of product (both produce and meat alike), but also the prices from competition are impossible for local families to match. Much of the existing food supply is quickly taken by the restaurants, and what little remains for locals is of poor quality at a high price. Given that an average Cuban makes the equivalent of US$25 a month, and US$45 for a professional job (like an engineer or a doctor), the price of dining at a paladar, where meals can cost just as much, is simply impossible. Cuba has always existed in an us-versus-them paradigm, and food is the surest proof that this continues to exist.

Unlike tourists, Cubans who can afford to eat outside of the home flock to inexpensive choices like the Coppelia ice cream parlors that flank the streets of Havana, and the cafeterias where locals and tourists alike can purchase meals for a few CUC (Cuban Convertible Peso).

Each Cuban is given a monthly ration book by the government for food, to provide for basics like rice and sugar, beans and eggs; however, these rations do not provide for meat or produce. The ration amount is sufficient for only twenty days or less, which is most often not enough to feed a family for the entire month, and it certainly does not include much in the way of protein.

Beef, an item served in most Cuban paladares, is tricky to come by. In 2003, the government declared it illegal to slaughter cattle without a government contract. This regulation means that government-run establishments have access to legal beef, while all others procure it on the black market.

Adding complication to an already difficult situation is a government that imposes capricious, shifting regulations for every aspect of economic life. Cuba's rules and regulations are constantly in flux, followed with extreme corruption and a prosperous black market that locals must depend on to live their daily lives. Even top restaurants depend on supplies from the black market in order to provide enough food for nightly guests.

Additionally, a main contributing factor to the current food shortage is the illogical and seemingly draconian regulation prohibiting farmers from the countryside from importing their goods into the capital's local markets. Only allowed to sell to private restaurants, farmers waste much of their produce, while the local people go without food. As with anything else in Cuba, enforcement is key to maintaining strict regulations, and there are considerable amounts of police patrolling the highways to ensure that this farm distribution cannot occur.

Markets are often empty of products, and residents may have to spend an entire day searching for something as basic and essential to their diet as chicken or pork. Government-run bakeries, grocery stores, and markets simply cannot sustain the demand with the current food production on the island that now includes an increasing tourist population to boot.

Why not fish from the bountiful sea, you ask? The Gulf of Mexico is home to marlin and the large fish called pargo (a prized local snapper). However, Cubans are forbidden from stepping foot onto any boat without express consent from the government, and those who are fortunate enough to have this luxurious privilege are very few and far between. Havana and San Juan, Puerto Rico, are the only major Caribbean ports situated on the Atlantic Ocean, and while the Havana harbor was once an ideal spot for boats, it is now too shallow for modern shipping vessels. Additionally, the majority of fishermen that remain are elderly; there is a consistent fuel shortage; and most of the working boats on the island left for Florida a long time ago.

* * *

While Cuba has some of the most untouched virgin, chemical-free soil on the earth, and the most pristine living coral reef known to man, its bounties are restricted by government policy and regulation, and the people of the island often are left with very little. When I last visited, I met a group of German farmers who had come to see if they could lend a hand. Each of the group represented a different farming interest and specialty, and they expressed frustration in what they had seen. In Germany, where growing something like potatoes is a simple feat, in Cuba the red tape is just too severe.

The *New York Times* reported that Juan Alejandro Trianro, an economist at the University of Havana, said, "The government has consistently failed to invest properly in the agriculture sector. We don't just have to feed eleven million people anymore. We have to feed more than fourteen million. In the next five years, if we don't do something about it, food will become a national security issue here."

* * *

While food in Cuba isn't nearly as diverse as that of more international Latin American or Caribbean cultures, the cuisine in restaurants is changing rapidly as owners and chefs are influenced by international visitors' ideas, and the newly-found global influences on Cuban cuisine are beginning to yield interesting results.

We can only hope that this resurgence of cuisine in Havana can bless the tables of the average home, and that the people's access to, and relationship with, food continues to grow. As additional restaurants flourish and sustain themselves through increased tourism, the demand for farming and produce will increase as well. One hopes that the overall population will in turn benefit in the bounty.

I was in Cuba during President Obama's easing of regulations and the landing of the first commercial flights from the US in more than fifty years. I arrived only hours after Fidel Castro's death and partook in his mesmerizing funeral, surrounded by a million grieving Cubans. I also stood arm in arm with my Cuban friends as the news of President Trump's travel restrictions were announced. Cuba's tourism is ever changing and rapidly evolving, but also slowing. It is an enigma, an energetic whirlwind, and the future is only a guess. Growth and transition foster the seed of invention and innovation, and food is often where these shifts begin.

* * *

Politics aside, the experience of visiting Cuba is as rich as one can experience while traveling through the world. As you explore Cuban Flavor, please move forward with sensitivity, and remember, in our excitement and enthusiasm for this culture's culinary history, and their newfound flavors, what a true and honest privilege it is to have access to food.

Practically speaking, recipes in this book are meals that can be made easily and with simple ingredients found at most stores in the US, and the recipes are perfect for a frugal budget and a hungry crowd. I hope you enjoy many of these recipes. From the succulent spiced meat of the Ropa Vieja, to the sweet and sticky arroz con leche, or the local favorite, sweet flan served in a soda can, Cuban cuisine has something for every palate. Havana is sweet, bitter, sour, and dirty—even perspiration takes on a character of its own. These beguiling Cuban flavors cannot be easily forgotten.

Pair these delights with a warm, sultry night, an old convertible, and a jazz band, and you just might fall deeply in love with the people, flavors, and beauty that is Cuba.

Liza Gershman

Stock Your Cuban Cupboard

Once you have a few essentials in your pantry, you can easily make almost any Cuban meal. Cuban food is simple, but delicious, and a few ingredients can combine into such a welcome variety of flavors. You will need both perishable and non-perishables to complete your cooking list, as well as a good saucepan, a large cutting board, sharp knives, a stock pot, a rice cooker, and a slow cooker.

Ancho
Olive oil
Yellow rice
White rice
Red beans
Black beans
Bijol
Bay leaves
Cumin
Salt
Pepper
Tomato paste
Canned stewed tomatoes
Garlic
Capers
Condensed milk
Cream of coconut
Cinnamon
Paprika
Star anise
Vanilla extract

Brown sugar
White sugar
Flour
White rum
Brown rum
Maraschino cherries
Guava paste
Sugarcane juice

PERISHABLES:

Red onions
White onions
Tomatoes
Red bell peppers
Green bell peppers
Green olives
Cilantro
Avocado
Mango
Papaya

Pineapple
Lemon
Lime
Lobster
Shrimp
Chicken breasts
Pork shoulder
Ground beef
Chorizo sausage
Swiss cheese
Jack cheese
Butter
Dry white wine
Red wine

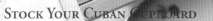

La Guarida

La Guarida, Cuba's most notable and beloved restaurant, is situated in the well-worn interior of Cuba's historic center. A former apartment building and ballet school, known as La Mansión Camagüey, it has been superbly reimagined and cared for by the proprietors, a husband-and-wife team, Enrique and Odeisys Nuñez. The couple have dedicated themselves to the perseverance of fine Cuban cuisine and a full modern-meets-classical restoration of the stunning structure, and they employ some fifty staff at their thriving restaurant.

The exterior is nothing significant: a relatively unmarked facade on a now derelict street; but the inside is magic. The marble staircase that was once the grand foyer still stands, and the airy second floor's high ceilings and elongated window arches always stop patrons on their way up for a sigh of awe. Fine table linens, German silver, and vintage chandeliers add to the sense of the interior's timelessness, and imagining Cuba in its heyday becomes very tangible.

Enrique Nuñez

Meals are delectable, and great care has been taken to meet the highest standards. Rich flavors from across the island mingle in simmering pots and scorching pans to offer guests delicacies such as rabbit pâté, oxtail risotto, and chocolate soufflé.

Much of La Guarida's success is truly because of Enrique's likeability and his considerable, apparent love for the building and the people he employs.

Enrique grew up in the building and remembers longing as a young boy to "make things better," as he told me while he puffed on one of Havana's finest cigars. From humble beginnings (a very small two-room apartment for his entire family), Enrique offered the space to the film crew of the independent film, *Fresa y Chocolate*. The film received international acclaim, and viewers encouraged Enrique to turn his home into a restaurant for all to enjoy.

Opened in 1996, La Guarida prides itself on offering an amalgamation of time: a memory of Cuba's past through the building, a moment in its present, and an eye to the future with an ever-changing cuisine.

carne

Papas Rellenas

FRIED STUFFED POTATO BALLS

Fried potato croquettes stuffed with flavorful picadillo (ground beef hash). Mouth-watering treats, when you can find them!

SERVINGS: ABOUT 25 POTATO BALLS

INGREDIENTS

4 LARGE POTATOES, PEELED AND CUBED	1 TSP PAPRIKA
½ TSP SALT	1 TSP DRIED OREGANO
1 TBSP WARM MILK	½ TSP SALT
1 TBSP VEGETABLE OIL	1 TSP FRESHLY CRACKED BLACK PEPPER
1 ONION, FINELY CHOPPED	1 TSP CUMIN
2 GARLIC CLOVES, PEELED AND CHOPPED	1 LIME, JUICED
1 LB GROUND SIRLOIN	2 EGGS
2 SMALL GREEN BELL PEPPERS, FINELY CHOPPED (ABOUT 1 CUP)	1 TBSP WATER
	1 CUP DRY BREADCRUMBS
2 SMALL RED BELL PEPPERS, FINELY CHOPPED (ABOUT 1 CUP)	¼ CUP ALL-PURPOSE FLOUR
1 TBSP WORCESTERSHIRE SAUCE	VEGETABLE OIL TO FILL THE PAN, FOR FRYING

PREPARATION

Boil potatoes until they are tender. Drain, then mash the potatoes with ½ tsp salt and warm milk. Let cool.

Next, make the filling. Heat a large pot over medium-high heat. Drizzle in 1 Tbsp vegetable oil, and add the finely chopped onion and garlic. Stir and cook until the onions are translucent and then add ground sirloin. Using a wooden spoon, break up the beef and allow it to cook until fully browned.

Add the green and red bell peppers. Stir and continue to cook. In a small bowl, mix together Worcestershire sauce, paprika, oregano, ½ tsp salt, pepper, cumin, and lime juice to form a paste. Season the beef mixture with the paste and stir thoroughly, cooking for 5 minutes more.

Remove from the heat and transfer to a bowl. Allow to cool completely.

Measure out a ball of the potato mixture onto the palm of your hand. Flatten out the ball into a flat circle with an indentation in the center. Stuff the indentation with the spiced beef mixture. Bring the sides together and smooth out to make a round ball. Continue with the rest of the potato and beef mixtures, until all the balls are formed.

In a bowl, whisk together the eggs and water. In another bowl, combine the breadcrumbs and the flour. Dip the ball into the beaten egg, and then roll in the flour mixture until lightly covered. Dip the ball in the egg again, and roll in the breadcrumbs again to coat thoroughly. Continue until each potato ball is coated twice, placing them on parchment-lined baking sheets.

It is very important to refrigerate the potato balls for 2–4 hours before proceeding to the next step.

Use a frying pan or a medium-size pot to fry the potato balls. Fill with enough oil to cover the potato balls. Heat oil to the frying stage (about 375°F) and drop about 4 potato balls into the hot oil. Let them cook for about 2–5 minutes or until golden brown. Turn the potato balls frequently to ensure even browning.

Transfer the fried potato balls to a plate lined with paper towels to drain off the excess oil.

Casa Miglis

Casa Miglis is my favorite way to start any visit to the island. Once you enter, you are surrounded by sound and scent, and each is decidedly Cuban. The decor is an interesting, eclectic mix, conveying the 1800s rather than the typically seen 1950s. The whitewashed wooden rooms of the rustic house and rickety floors lead the way to a small stage at the back featuring a vibrant musical group, trumpeting out island rhythms and salsa music, with help from a stand-up bass, maracas, classical guitar, and bongo drums.

The food comes from local producers, and like most other food in Cuba, it is organic. Miglis, owned by a Swedish man named Michael, has an unusual menu that is heavy on dairy and that combines regional spices with European flavors. The cheeses are imported because they aren't readily accessible on the island (cheese isn't typically a part of the local Cuban diet). Ceviche, bruschetta, gazpacho, Greek souvlaki, Mexican lamb chili, spaghetti with cream sauce, stuffed chicken breast, and rum ice cream are just a few of the offerings on the list.

Cuban music is one of the richest and most influential regional music cultures of the world, with its unique sounds and styles derived from West African and European (particularly Spanish) traditions. Cuban music is vast and encompasses a multitude of genres.

Ajiaco

CUBAN SOUP

Thought to originate from the native Taíno people of the island of Cuba, this stew-like soup is traditionally made at the start of the San Juan festival in the city of Camagüey. Surprisingly enough, the temperature in Cuba drops to the low 50s several times a year, and a warm soup is perfect for the mild weather. The first time I experienced this relative chill, I was so taken by surprise that I had nothing warm enough to wear. I layered almost everything that I had with me and am sure I looked truly bizarre. This soup would have been the exact remedy for the cold.

SERVES 4–6
INGREDIENTS

STEW:

¼ LB FLANK STEAK, CUBED INTO BITE-SIZE PIECES

½ LB PORK LOIN, CUBED INTO BITE-SIZE PIECES

4 CUPS CHICKEN BROTH

¼ CUP RED WINE

¼ CUP BONIATO (SWEET POTATO), PEELED AND CUBED

¼ CUP YUCA (CASSAVA), PEELED AND CUBED

¼ CUP FRESH PUMPKIN (OR BUTTERNUT SQUASH), PEELED AND CUBED

1 RIPE PLANTAIN, PEELED AND CUBED

1 EAR OF FRESH SWEET CORN, HUSKED AND CUT INTO 2-INCH CHUNKS

1 TSP SALT

½ TSP PEPPER

2 TSP PAPRIKA

1 BAY LEAF

1 FRESH LIME, CUT INTO SLICES

SOFRITO:

3 TBSP OLIVE OIL

1 SMALL ONION, DICED

¼ GREEN PEPPER, DICED

2 CLOVES FRESH GARLIC, MINCED

1 CAN (8 OZ) TOMATO SAUCE

½ TSP CUMIN

½ TSP OREGANO

PREPARATION

Place the stew ingredients, except the lime, into a 6-quart Crock-Pot.

For the sofrito, heat olive oil in a saucepan over medium heat. Cook the onion and green pepper until the onion is translucent. Add in the garlic, tomato sauce, cumin, and oregano.

Add this mixture to the Crock-Pot with the stew. Cook on low for 6–8 hours.

Remove the bay leaf, squeeze in lime juice, and serve while hot.

Bistec De Palomilla

BUTTERFLIED BEEFSTEAK

When beef is available to Cubans, it is often tough and of poor quality. This recipe is a typical Cuban dish that uses thinly sliced meat pounded with a mallet to tenderize the beef. The majority of the beef raised on the island comes from the countryside near Trinidad, and is regulated by the government. It is currently illegal to sell beef outside of state-run restaurants and hotels. When available to locals, beef is sometimes sold on the black market, and more rarely available at the local market. Cubans often substitute pork in any recipe that calls for beef.

INGREDIENTS

3 LB TOP SIRLOIN STEAK, SLICED VERY THIN

10 GARLIC CLOVES, DICED

SALT AND COARSE BLACK PEPPER, TO TASTE

2 FRESH LIMES

1 YELLOW ONION, THINLY SLICED

OLIVE OIL, SWIRLED TWICE AROUND THE PAN

3 TBSP FRESHLY CHOPPED PARSLEY

SERVE WITH:

BLACK BEANS AND YELLOW RICE

PREPARATION

Thoroughly rub both sides of the sirloin with garlic, salt, and pepper, and set garlic aside. Squeeze the juice from 1 lime onto the meat. Place the uncooked sirloin in a covered bowl, and add the sliced raw onion. Refrigerate for a minimum of one hour to allow the flavors to marinate and the meat to tenderize. The longer you marinate, the better the flavor, and marinating overnight in the refrigerator is suggested if time allows.

When ready, remove the steaks from the marinade and pat dry, reserving the juicy marinade for later. Set the onions aside as well.

Heat olive oil in a large frying pan and place in the meat, frying the steaks quickly (no more than 1 minute per side), then remove and place on a warm platter.

In the same pan, add the remaining marinade, onions, garlic, and lime juice from the remaining 1 lime, and quickly stir together over medium heat for approximately 5 minutes. Remove this light sauce from the heat while the onions are still crisp and the garlic is white.

Drizzle the onion mixture over the steaks as a sauce, and garnish with a sprinkling of chopped fresh parsley.

Serve with black beans and yellow rice.

POT ROAST

Pot roast, like many other slow-cooked recipes, is a throwback to the 1950s culture that lingers in Cuba. This dish is particularly common on the rare occasion when Cubans do have access to beef. The slow-roasting process tenderizes the meat, which is typically tougher than the meat we find in the United States.

INGREDIENTS

4 LB CHUCK OR RUMP ROAST (SLOW COOKING WILL MAKE IT FORK-TENDER)

FLOUR, TO DUST

8 CLOVES GARLIC, MINCED

SALT AND PEPPER, TO TASTE

1½ TSP DRIED OREGANO

½ CUP OLIVE OIL

2 LARGE YELLOW ONIONS, THICKLY SLICED

2 CUPS BEEF STOCK

1 CAN (8 OZ) TOMATO SAUCE

1 CUP NARANJA AGRIA (BITTER ORANGE MARINADE)

1 CUP DRY WHITE WINE

1 CUP SMALL RED POTATOES

¼ CUP GREEN PIMIENTO-STUFFED OLIVES, WITH LIQUID

3 BAY LEAVES

PREPARATION

Pat the roast dry and lightly flour.

Mash minced garlic, salt, pepper, and oregano together in a mortar to form a thick paste. Generously rub the roast with the garlic paste.

Heat a large skillet with a coating of olive oil and add the roast, browning on all sides. Tongs will help this process. Once the roast is nicely browned, remove from the skillet and place into your crockpot.

In the same skillet that you used to brown the meat, cook the onions until translucent. Remove the onions and layer them over the roast inside the crockpot. Cover the roast with beef stock, tomato sauce, naranja agria, and white wine. Add in the potatoes, olives, and bay leaves.

Cook the mixture on a low setting for 6–8 hours. Remove bay leaves. Serve the roast with the potatoes, onions, and olives.

Carne Con Papas

MEAT WITH POTATOES

Another slow-cooked recipe, carne con papas, is served in many Cuban restaurants. This flavorful dish is similar to a stew. The best on the island is served at the Finca Agroecologica El Paraiso in the countryside of Viñales. The feast there is abundant, and the carne comes to the table after pumpkin soup, salads, chicken, fish, and pork. It takes a few visits to get the eating pace just-so to save room for the carne con papas, but it is worth the practice. Savory, rich, and warm, the flavors of this hearty dish are among my favorites.

INGREDIENTS

4 CUPS BEEF BOUILLON (6 CUBES)	2 TBSP BIJOL
4 CUPS WATER	2 BAY LEAVES
OLIVE OIL, FOR STIR-FRYING	1 CAN (8 OZ) TOMATO SAUCE
½ SMALL WHITE ONION, CHOPPED	1 CAN (14.5 OZ) DICED TOMATOES
½ GREEN BELL PEPPER, SEEDED AND CHOPPED	2 LB BEEF STEW MEAT
3 CLOVES GARLIC, CRUSHED	2 WHITE POTATOES, CUT INTO SMALL CUBES
½ TSP GROUND CUMIN	1 CUP DRY WHITE WINE
¼ TSP SALT	**SERVE WITH:**
¼ TSP PEPPER	WHITE RICE AND FRESH SALAD

PREPARATION

Make a stock with 6 cubes beef bouillon and 4 cups water.

In a medium skillet, heat olive oil and add in the onion, green pepper, and garlic. Sauté the mix until the onion is translucent and the garlic softens.

Add in the cumin, salt, pepper, bijol, and bay leaves. Cook for 1-2 minutes before adding in the tomato sauce and let the ingredients marry by cooking them for another 1 minute to heat through.

Add the beef stock, the sauce, and the remaining ingredients to the Crock-Pot, and cook the mix on a low setting for 6-8 hours or overnight as the flavors combine. This slow cooking is key to really bring out the flavors of the dish.

When finished, serve over a heaping side of white rice along with fresh salad.

Criollo-Style Minced Meat

Cuban creole cuisine stems from the 1800s, when French slave owners migrated to Cuba from Haiti to escape the revolution and brought with them more than 27,000 Haitian slaves. After Spanish, Creole is the second most spoken language on the island, and traditions from the Haitian culture have become so indelibly woven into Cuban culture that they are impossible to separate out. Religion, music, and food all express Cuba's deep Creole roots, and this dish's minced ingredients are a perfect metaphor for Cuba's blended culture.

INGREDIENTS

16 oz ground or minced beef

Salt and pepper, to taste

Oil, for the pan

4 Tbsp red pepper

4 Tbsp criollo seasoning (found in any major grocery store)

8 dashes of parsley, minced

PREPARATION

Season the beef with salt and pepper.

Stir-fry beef in a frying pan with hot oil until the fat separates off. Once this happens, reduce the heat, add red pepper and criollo seasoning, and cook for approximately 5 minutes more.

Sprinkle with parsley and serve.

Pastel de Chorizo

CHORIZO PIE

Similar to an empanada but larger, the aromas of sautéed onion, cumin, and ancho chili from an almost-baked chorizo pie are enough to draw a crowd to the kitchen. While you typically find this dish in restaurants, chorizo pie was a party favorite when beef was commonly available in Cuba before the Special Period.

Serves 12-14 (MAKES TWO 9-INCH PIES)

INGREDIENTS

1½ CUPS CHOPPED YELLOW ONION

4 CLOVES GARLIC, MINCED

2 CUPS RED OR GREEN PEPPER, CHOPPED

4 TBSP BUTTER

1 LB CHORIZO SAUSAGE

14 EXTRA LARGE EGGS

1 PINT HEAVY CREAM

¾ TSP SALT

½ TSP PEPPER

1 TSP GROUND CUMIN

1½ TSP ANCHO CHILI POWDER

2 UNBAKED PIE CRUSTS (CAN BE PREMADE)

2 CUPS GRATED JACK CHEESE

PARSLEY, TO GARNISH

PREPARATION

Preheat oven to 450°F.

Sauté the onion, garlic, and green pepper in butter until translucent. Remove the chorizo from its casing and brown with the mixture. Once cooked through, drain off the excess fat. Set aside.

Beat eggs in a mixing bowl until frothy. Gradually add cream, salt, pepper, cumin, and chili powder. Combine the chorizo mixture with the egg mixture and spread an even layer on the bottom of each pie shell. Top with grated cheese.

Bake for the first 10 minutes at 450°F. Reduce oven temperature to 300°F and continue baking until the custard sets, about 45-50 minutes. Garnish with parsley.

Croquetas de Jamón

HAM CROQUETTES

Croquetas de jamón are a common starter in local and fine dining restaurants around the island. Served piping hot, the bite-size morsels of deep-fried goodness are best made in the kitchen of La Guarida, but you can even get them at the airport on your departure if you find that you just haven't had enough!

SERVINGS: 20–24 CROQUETAS

INGREDIENTS

8 OZ COOKED HAM, CUBED

1 TBSP DIJON MUSTARD

3 TBSP UNSALTED BUTTER

¼ CUP UNBLEACHED ALL-PURPOSE FLOUR, PLUS MORE FOR DUSTING

1½ CUPS WHOLE MILK

KOSHER SALT AND FRESHLY GROUND PEPPER, TO TASTE

PINCH OF FRESHLY GROUND NUTMEG

½ CUP FLOUR

2 LARGE EGGS, WELL BEATEN, ROOM TEMPERATURE

1 CUP DRIED BREADCRUMBS

CANOLA OIL, FOR DEEP-FRYING

PREPARATION

Combine ham and mustard in a food processor, and pulse until they form a smooth paste.

Melt the butter in a heavy saucepan over medium-low heat. Gradually add in ¼ cup flour and cook while stirring constantly until well blended, but not browned. This mixture will become what is commonly known as béchamel.

As the butter melts, heat the milk to a simmer in a different pan, but do not let it boil. Add the milk to the butter mixture, whisking constantly until the béchamel sauce has thickened and is pulling away from the sides of the pan. Remove the sauce from the heat. Gently add in the pureed ham and mix until it is thoroughly combined. Season with salt, pepper, and nutmeg to taste.

Pour the mixture onto a lined baking sheet. Bring the mix to room temperature and cover and refrigerate until it sets, for at least 1 hour (but you can chill overnight).

Place flour, beaten eggs, and breadcrumbs in different mixing bowls. Spoon the béchamel mixture into walnut-sized pieces and roll into the desired shape. Roll each croqueta in flour, gently drop them one at a time into the egg mixture, and transfer to the breadcrumbs. The croquetas should be completely coated in breadcrumbs.

Add about 3 inches of oil to a large heavy skillet over medium-high heat (about 375°F). Add the croquetas in small batches, being careful not to break them as you go. Turn until brown on all sides, about 2 minutes. Remove and drain on paper towels and serve warm.

Croquetas de Jamón y Queso

HAM AND CHEESE CROQUETTES

The few cows on the island mean little access to cheese, and this melty dish is certainly a delicacy found only on restaurant menus, and not in households.

SERVINGS: 20–24 CROQUETAS

INGREDIENTS

8 oz smoked ham, excess fat or rind trimmed, cubed

1 Tbsp Dijon mustard

4 Tbsp unsalted butter

½ cup shallots, minced

2 Tbsp unbleached all-purpose flour

1 cup whole milk

½ cup grated Gruyère or Emmental cheese

Kosher salt and freshly ground pepper, to taste

⅛ tsp freshly ground nutmeg

Pinch of pimentón (optional)

½ cup unbleached all-purpose flour

2 large eggs, well beaten

1½ cups dried breadcrumbs (or cracker meal), finely ground

Sunflower oil, for deep frying

PREPARATION

Combine ham and mustard in a food processor and pulse until it forms a smooth paste.

Melt the butter in a heavy saucepan over medium-low heat. Add the shallots and sauté until translucent.

Add 2 Tbsp flour and cook, stirring constantly until well blended but not browned, about 2 minutes. In the meantime, in a different pot, gently heat the milk to a simmer, but do not let it boil.

Gradually stir the heated milk into the saucepan, whisking constantly to eliminate clumps. Stir until the sauce has thickened and the whisk leaves trace marks in the surface, about 5 minutes.

Stir in cheese and season with salt, pepper, nutmeg, and pimentón to complete the béchamel sauce. Remove from heat. Add the pureed ham and mix until well combined.

Bring to room temperature. Pour the mixture in a shallow bowl or lined baking sheet. Cover with plastic wrap and refrigerate until set, at least 1 hour.

Lay out ½ cup flour, beaten eggs, and breadcrumbs in separate mixing bowls. Scoop out 1 heaping Tbsp of the béchamel mixture and roll each croqueta in the flour to coat, shaking off the excess flour. Dip into the egg mixture with a fork or slotted spoon, allowing excess to drip off, and then roll in breadcrumbs. They should be well coated so the filling doesn't leak when cooked.

Add about 3 inches of oil to a large, deep pot. Heat over medium-high heat to 365°F. Working in batches, carefully add the croquetas a few at a time. Do not crowd them, or the temperature of the oil will drop. Gently turn until brown on all sides, about 2 minutes.

Remove with a slotted spoon and drain on paper towels or re-purposed grocery paper bags. Bring the oil back up to the correct temperature in between batches. Serve immediately.

THE CUBAN SANDWICH

Although the Cuban sandwich is not usually found in Cuba, when it is on a menu, the flavors are a refreshing turn from the more common grilled cheese or jamón y queso (ham and cheese). The pickle planks and mustard are difficult to come by, and most markets don't carry them now, but when put in a sandwich they add an unmistakably Cuban zest. The best place for a Cubano is the lively Callejon de Hamel in Havana on Sunday afternoons. If you can withstand the crowds and arrive early enough, this alley of street art and Afro-Caribbean-influenced shops is the best place to learn about the religion Santería and its traditions. While Cuba doesn't have official food carts, the local chef on the street has his own version of a Cubano stand, with all of the fixings and a smile you won't soon forget.

SERVES 4

INGREDIENTS

1 LOAF CUBAN BREAD

4 TBSP UNSALTED BUTTER, SOFTENED

8 SLICES SWISS OR JACK CHEESE (ABOUT ½ LB)

¼ CUP YELLOW MUSTARD

16 SLICES MAPLE-GLAZED HONEY HAM (ABOUT 1 LB)

16 SLICES HOT CAPICOLA (ABOUT 1LB)

8–12 SLICES SWEET DILL PICKLE PLANKS

PREPARATION

You can use a panini press, a sauté pan, or a grill—just like the chef on Hamel does. If you are using a panini press, preheat to medium-high.

Layer the bread with butter, cheese, and mustard.

On one half of each sandwich, layer 4 slices of maple-glazed honey ham and 4 slices of capicola.

Add 2–3 pickle planks on top of the meat and close the sandwich.

Place the sandwich in the panini press, grill, or sauté pan (medium-high heat), and put something heavy and heat proof on top. You want to really bond the layers together to bring out the flavor.

Cook until the cheese is melted and the outside is slightly charred and crisped, which will take about 5 minutes

Cuban Spiced Pork Chops

A typical dish found in most paladares, these tender and flavorful chops use many of the island's most common ingredients in a lean, easy-to-cook dish: cumin, garlic, and lime. I love riding horses out into the countryside of Trinidad and stopping at some of the local ranchóns (ranches) for lunch, where there is always something delicious to eat straight from the grill. Some of my most memorable Cuban experiences come from sitting under the unassuming thatched roofs at a ranchón, listening to the local farmers play the guitar, drinking fresh sugar cane juice, and eating freshly grilled pork.

SERVES 2
INGREDIENTS

2 LEAN BONELESS PORK CHOPS	¼ TSP FRESH GROUND PEPPER
2 LIMES, JUICED	½ TSP OLIVE OIL (OPTIONAL)
½ TSP GROUND CUMIN	**SERVE WITH:**
2 GARLIC CLOVES, CRUSHED	RICE AND PLANTAINS
¼ TSP ONION POWDER	

PREPARATION

Trim the excess fat from the pork chops, and cut shallow cross-hatch marks on both sides of the meat.

Mix all remaining ingredients together in a bowl. Add in the chops and allow them to soak. Cover and place in the refrigerator to chill and marinate for a minimum of 1 hour.

Once chilled, grill or broil the chops at 500°F for 8–10 minutes, turning over halfway through. To maximize the tenderness of the meat and juices in the chops, only flip the meat once.

Serve with a side of rice and plantains.

Lechon Asado

CUBAN MOJO MARINATED PORK

The centerpiece dish of Cuban celebrations is the lechon (whole pig). While visiting the small tree-lined lake in Las Terrazas, an hour and a half outside of Havana in Cuba's countryside, I stumbled on a family that was roasting a lechon on an open fire, and I've never forgotten the flavor. The Cuban spin on the traditional Latin-American dish is the mojo criollo, a marinade made from tangy citrus juice, cumin, oregano, and an abundance of garlic.

SERVES 6
INGREDIENTS

¾ CUP EXTRA-VIRGIN OLIVE OIL

1 TBSP ORANGE ZEST

¾ CUP FRESH ORANGE JUICE

½ CUP FRESH LIME JUICE

1 CUP CILANTRO, FINELY CHOPPED

¼ CUP LIGHTLY PACKED MINT LEAVES, FINELY CHOPPED

8 GARLIC CLOVES, MINCED

1 TBSP MINCED FRESH OREGANO (OR 2 TSP DRIED OREGANO)

2 TSP GROUND CUMIN

3½ LB BONELESS PORK SHOULDER, IN ONE PIECE *

KOSHER SALT AND PEPPER, TO TASTE

SERVE WITH:

FRIED OR SWEET PLANTAINS

RICE AND BEANS

PREPARATION

In a large bowl, combine olive oil, orange zest, orange juice, lime juice, cilantro, mint, garlic, oregano, and cumin. Mix, then add the pork shoulder to marinade. Cover and refrigerate overnight.

Preheat the oven to 425°F. Place a wire oven rack over a rimmed baking sheet.

Remove the pork from the marinade and season thoroughly with salt and pepper. Place the pork on the rack. Roast for 30 minutes until lightly browned. Turn the heat down to 375°F , and roast for another 1 hour and 20–30 minutes, or until a meat thermometer reads 160°F.

Transfer the pork to a cutting board and cover with aluminum foil, letting it rest for 20 or so minutes. Carve the pork against the grain and serve with a side of fried or sweet plantains and rice and beans.

*Note: even if you don't have access to a whole pig or the time to roast it, this recipe will still give you a similar flavor—in a more manageable size.

Fried Pork Chops

Easy to make and flavorful, fried pork chops are a Cuban staple.

INGREDIENTS

1.2 LB PORK CHOPS

SALT AND PEPPER, TO TASTE

¼ CLOVE GARLIC, CRUSHED

2 TBSP SOUR ORANGE JUICE

½ CUP OIL

8 TBSP ONION SEASONING

8 DASHES OF PARSLEY, MINCED

PREPARATION

Wrap the raw pork chops inside a damp cloth and lightly pound to tenderize. When tender, thoroughly season with salt and pepper, garlic, and sour orange juice.

Refrigerate and let the seasoning marinate for 3-4 hours. Heat oil in a frying pan and fry the chops until browned on both sides.

Serve with the onion seasoning and parsley on top.

Pernil Relleno de Moros y Cristianos

PORK PINWHEELS STUFFED WITH BLACK BEANS AND WHITE RICE

Found at fine dining restaurants on the island, these pinwheels are a typical Cuban dish.

SERVING SIZE: 6

INGREDIENTS

MARINADE:

1 CUP OLIVE OIL

½ CUP SOUR ORANGE JUICE

10 CLOVES GARLIC, CHOPPED

½ TSP OREGANO

SALT AND FRESHLY GROUND BLACK
    PEPPER, TO TASTE

6- TO 8-LB BONE-IN FRESH HAM OR PORK
    SHOULDER (4 CUPS)

MOROS Y CRISTIANOS:

4 CLOVES GARLIC, PEELED AND CRUSHED

3 TSP SALT

¼ LB BACON (ABOUT 6 STRIPS), CHOPPED

2 TBSP OLIVE OIL

1 ONION, FINELY CHOPPED (ABOUT 1 CUP)

1 GREEN PEPPER, SEEDED AND FINELY
    CHOPPED (ABOUT ¾ CUP)

1 BAY LEAF

¼ TSP GROUND CUMIN

½ TSP DRIED OREGANO

1½ CUPS LONG-GRAIN WHITE RICE

2 CANS (15.5 OZ EACH) BLACK BEANS,
    NOT DRAINED

1¾ CUPS WATER

1 TBSP RED WINE VINEGAR

CILANTRO, TO GARNISH

PREPARATION

In a small bowl, combine marinade ingredients except the meat, and let stand for 1 hour.

While the marinade sits, cut the pork lengthwise and remove the bone. Making small cuts, spread the meat until it is flat and can be trimmed into a rectangular shape. Discard excess fat. Transfer the meat to a shallow pan and pour the marinade over evenly. Refrigerate for at least 2 hours.

Prepare the Moros y Cristianos. Place garlic in a small bowl and sprinkle 1 tsp salt on top. Let sit for a few minutes before mixing into a paste. Set aside.

In a large pot over medium heat, add the bacon and olive oil, sautéing until the bacon fat turns golden brown, approximately 6 minutes. Stir occasionally to prevent it from sticking to the pot.

In the same pan, add the onion, green pepper, and garlic paste to the bacon and sauté until soft and translucent, approximately 5 minutes. Add the remaining 2 tsp salt, bay leaf, cumin, oregano, and rice and stir for approximately 1 minute until well combined and the rice is lightly coated in oil.

Pour the black beans and their liquid into the pot. Add in the water and vinegar. Cover the mixture and bring the pot to boil, then reduce to a simmer. Cook for 35–40 minutes, or until all the water has been absorbed by the rice. Remove from heat and let sit for 5 minutes before fluffing the rice with a fork. Garnish with cilantro.

Preheat the oven to 375°F. Spread Moros y Cristianos down the center of the meat and roll the meat over the rice mixture stuffing to fully enclose. Tie with cooking twine in a cross tie to secure.

Roast for 20 minutes per pound of pork used or until the inside temperature reaches 150°F. Use a thermometer to check that the meat is thoroughly cooked.

Atelier

On any given day in the mid-century, modern-inspired neighborhood of Miramar, you will find Niuris Ysabel Higueras Martinez hard at work in her globally-recognized restaurant, Atelier.

Niuris exudes joy with her boisterous laughter and larger-than-life smile. She knows that her hard work has paid off, and she has become one of Cuba's most recognized female entrepreneurs and restaurateurs.

Niuris opened the restaurant in 2010 and attributes much of her success to her passion and connection with her staff. "If you have the possibility to create a place with passion and soul, and you do this with love, then it isn't that difficult," she told me as we drank mineral water, sweating from the hot heat of the sun on the balcony of Atelier. "The challenge," she continued, "is how to maintain this. When I travel abroad, everything I bring home is for the restaurant: salt, pepper, and spices all come from the United States, and even our pans and knives and pastry bags, too." Like most, Atelier suffers from limited access to product and supplies, but Niurius's positive outlook shines through as she gleams that those challenges have served her restaurant well as they have "necessitated creativity." The creativity that Atelier offers is well noted by critics and patrons alike.

Creativity in the kitchen of Atelier largely stems from head chef Michael Voss. Inspired by international cuisine, Voss studied in Paris. "Sous vide changed my life," he said, as we gobbled up the family meal before the dinner seating. "I'm very optimistic about Cuba's food and the development of exciting cuisine here." Voss's flavors range from local to foreign, serving duck confit, lobster, and the beloved island favorite, ropa vieja.

For Niuris, the future is filled with hope. "I think that everything we need will come with time," she said, smiling. "We need market stability, and that is essential to our future. We have to constantly innovate, and that's what keeps us alive." Whether Niuris was talking specifically about Atelier or not, her sentiment couldn't be a more perfect metaphor for Cuba as well.

Cuban-Style Picadillo

Picadillo is a very traditional dish. While beef is difficult to come by in Cuba, you can find it on occasion at the markets. The exact recipe can change depending on what's available in the house or the market on any given day, but the base stays the same. Some days, you may find cayenne rather than cumin, others you might have red wine vinegar rather than red wine. Either way, the scent alone of this dish is enough to warm the stomachs of your guests, and leftovers are unlikely.

SERVING SIZE: 3
INGREDIENTS

¼ CUP OLIVE OIL

1 LARGE WHITE ONION, CHOPPED

8 GARLIC CLOVES, MINCED

6 TURKISH BAY LEAVES

2 LB GROUND BEEF (15 TO 20 PERCENT FAT)

1 CAN (14.5 OZ) DICED TOMATOES IN JUICE

¾ CUP RAISINS

¾ CUP SLICED AND DRAINED PIMIENTO-STUFFED GREEN OLIVES (FROM 5-OZ JAR)

¼ CUP TOMATO PASTE

1½ TSP RED WINE

1 TSP CHILI POWDER

¼ TSP CUMIN PEPPER

1 RED PEPPER, DICED

⅓ CUP CAPERS

SALT AND PEPPER, TO TASTE

SPRINKLING OF CILANTRO

SERVE WITH:

RICE AND FRESH LETTUCE

PREPARATION

Heat oil in a large pot over high heat until it sizzles. Add onion, garlic, and bay leaves. Sauté for approximately 5 minutes until the onion softens.

Add in the ground beef and break up into small pieces to mix with the ingredients. Sauté until browned on the outside and cooked on the inside. Drain the excess fat from the meat.

Mix in the rest of the ingredients except the salt, pepper, and cilantro. Simmer on low until the mixture thickens. Stir occasionally for approximately 8 minutes. Add in desired salt and pepper, and remove bay leaves. Top with a sprinkling of cilantro. Pour over rice and a bed of fresh lettuce, or serve on its own.

Refried Beans with Chorizo

A tasty side-dish substitution for the ubiquitous arroz con morro
(rice with black beans).

SERVES 4

INGREDIENTS

1 CAN (15.5 OZ) CANNELLINI OR PINTO BEANS

¼ LB GROUND CHORIZO

¼ CUP OLIVE OIL

½ MEDIUM ONION, CHOPPED

2 GARLIC CLOVES, CHOPPED

1 CHORIZO IN LINKS, SLICED

CUMIN, TO TASTE

SALT AND PEPPER, TO TASTE

PREPARATION

Bring beans to a boil in a saucepan. Strain the excess liquid and discard. Pour the cooked beans into a bowl and mash with a fork; set aside.

In the same pan, brown the ground chorizo. Drain the excess fat, and add the mashed beans, cooking until warmed through.

In a separate pan, heat oil and sauté the onion until translucent. Add the garlic, cooking until softened. Then add the sliced chorizo and cumin, salt, and pepper to taste. Combine with the mashed beans mixture and return to the saucepan to fry with the other ingredients until thoroughly warmed.

Roast Chicken

Like so many ingredients in Cuba, the availability of something as seemingly normal as chicken cannot be taken for granted. I've gone from store to store with my local friends in search of poultry, only to be turned away because of scarcity. When you do find chicken, it is guaranteed to be free-range and organic (like everything on the island), and because of that it offers a flavor that can be more sumptuous than what one often finds in the US.

Almost every Cuban kitchen has a slow cooker (a holdover from the 1950s).

INGREDIENTS

1.5 LB CHICKEN	1 TSP CUMIN
SALT AND PEPPER, TO TASTE	6 TBSP DRY WHITE WINE
8 DASHES OREGANO	1 ONION, SLICED
14 CLOVES GARLIC	4 TSP OIL
4 TSP SOUR ORANGE JUICE	

PREPARATION

Cut the chicken in eighths and marinate with salt, pepper, oregano, garlic, sour orange juice, cumin, and white wine.

Place the onions in an oiled pot. Add the chicken pieces on top of the onions. Cook over low heat and frequently brush with the juices. Continue cooking until the chicken is cooked through and tender.

Roasted Pork with Mango Glaze

Mango season in Cuba is something to celebrate! Fresh fruits drop from trees like gifts from the gods, even on the city streets. Locals and tourists alike eat mango straight off the branch. Any recipe that calls for lush, sweet mango is worth making, and adding mango to a pork dish is the perfect complement.

SERVES 12

INGREDIENTS

½ LARGE MANGO, PEELED AND CUT INTO ½-INCH CHUNKS (1 CUP)

2 TBSP SUGAR

1½ TSP TAMARIND PASTE

½ TSP SOY SAUCE

¼ TSP CRUSHED RED PEPPER

½ TSP VEGETABLE OIL

1 GARLIC CLOVE, MINCED

SALT AND FRESHLY GROUND PEPPER, TO TASTE

1 PORK LOIN ROAST (4 LB), TIED

EXTRA-VIRGIN OLIVE OIL, FOR THE PAN

½ CUP DRY WHITE WINE

¾ CUP CHICKEN STOCK OR LOW-SODIUM BROTH

PREPARATION

Preheat the oven to 300°F. Combine the mango with sugar, tamarind paste, soy sauce, and crushed red pepper in a blender until the mixture is pureed and smooth.

Heat the oil in a pan and cook the garlic until fragrant. Add the mango puree to the pan and season with salt and pepper. Bring the pan to a simmer and cook over low heat until the mixture thickens, approximately 5 minutes.

Thoroughly cover both sides of the pork roast with salt and pepper. Add the roast to a new warmed, oiled skillet and cook over high heat, turning occasionally, until it is browned all over, approximately 7 minutes.

Move the skillet to the oven and roast the pork for approximately 45 minutes, until it is cooked through. Brush the mango glaze generously and evenly over the roast. Continue to roast for another 5–7 minutes.

Light the broiler, and brush additional mango glaze and pan drippings over the pork. Broil 8 inches from the heat for 5 minutes, or until the glaze is a bit sticky and golden. Transfer the roast to a cutting board and let rest for 15 minutes before slicing.

While waiting for the roast to rest, pour out the fat from the skillet and set the skillet on the stove top over moderately high heat. Add the wine and cook. Transfer to a small saucepan and simmer the jus until reduced by half for approximately 5 minutes. Add the chicken stock and simmer until slightly reduced, for 3 minutes longer. Season the jus with a generous amount of salt and pepper.

Ropa Vieja

"RAGS"

The national dish of Cuba, "rags" or ropa vieja, is savory and delectable. When spices are few and far between, this dish's peppers bring forward a wonderfully light flavor. Traditional ropa vieja is made with flank steak because that cut of beef is best for shredding, but a more flavorful top sirloin works just as well.

SERVES 6

INGREDIENTS

2 LB FLANK STEAK	½ TSP DRIED OREGANO
SALT AND PEPPER, TO TASTE	½ TSP CUMIN POWDER
1 YELLOW ONION, DICED	1 BAY LEAF
1 TSP GARLIC, MINCED	½ CUP GREEN OLIVES, HALVED
1 CAN (28 OZ) DICED TOMATOES	2 TSP CAPERS (OPTIONAL)
½ CUP WATER	1 TBSP CILANTRO, CHOPPED (OPTIONAL)
1 RED BELL PEPPER, THINLY SLICED	**SERVE WITH:**
1 GREEN BELL PEPPER, THINLY SLICED	RICE
1 JALAPEÑO, SEEDED AND THINLY SLICED	

PREPARATION

Generously season the flank steak with salt and pepper.

Combine onion, garlic, tomatoes and their juices, water, bell peppers, jalapeño, oregano, cumin, and bay leaf in a slow cooker. Add the flank steak, cover, and cook on low for 8 hours.

Remove the meat and let it rest approximately 10 minutes. Discard the bay leaf and stir in the olives, capers (optional), and cilantro (optional).

Shred the meat into fine strips and add it back into the sauce. Season with salt and pepper to taste.

Serve hot over a bed of rice.

Vaca Frita

CRISPY BEEF

A similar dish to the Cuban favorite ropa vieja, vaca frita (literally "fried cow") is equally loved. Rather than the stewed tomato mixture in the classic ropa, this dish combines the tangy flavors of citrus with garlic and salt.

SERVES 6
INGREDIENTS

1½ LB FLANK STEAK, CUT INTO 4 PIECES

SALT, TO COAT MEAT

WATER, TO BOIL

1 GREEN BELL PEPPER, CORED AND QUARTERED

1 LARGE ONION, HALVED

1 BAY LEAF

2 GARLIC CLOVES, SMASHED

½ TSP SALT

¼ CUP + 2 TBSP FRESH LIME JUICE

3 TBSP EXTRA-VIRGIN OLIVE OIL

1 LARGE ONION, SLICED

OIL, TO STIR-FRY

SALT AND FRESHLY GROUND PEPPER, TO TASTE

SERVE WITH:

YELLOW OR WHITE RICE

PREPARATION

Coat the raw flank steak with salt and place in a large pot, adding enough water to cover it fully. Bring to a boil. Add in the bell pepper, halved onion, and bay leaf.

Simmer the mix over moderate heat for approximately 20 minutes. Once the ingredients finish simmering, take out the flank steak and let cool. Strain the broth and save for another recipe. Shred the meat with a fork or your fingers, and transfer to a bowl.

Mash the garlic to a paste and add ½ tsp salt. Combine the garlic salt paste and the lime juice, olive oil, and remaining sliced onion. Coat the meat with the mixture. Let stand at room temperature for at least 30 minutes.

Pour oil into a pan and let sizzle. Once the temperature is hot enough for frying, add the shredded beef and season with salt and pepper to taste. Cook over high heat, turning once, until the meat sizzles and crisps. This should take approximately 6 minutes on the stove.

Serve hot over a bed of yellow or white rice.

pollo

Arroz con Pollo

RICE WITH CHICKEN

Arroz con pollo is one of the most common dishes served at home. Sometimes a side dish and sometimes the main meal, its sticky, saucy texture and flavors are ubiquitous in both the Cuban household and fine dining kitchens. The dish, with its sprinkling of black or red kidney beans, is a main staple of the Cuban diet. One of the most delectable arroz con pollos on the island is made in the kitchen of the local favorite Las Dueñas. Served in an earthenware dish as an individual serving with piping-hot saffron steam, this meal is something I long for during every visit. Las Dueñas, located on an unassuming street in the neighborhood of Vedado, is a six-table indoor-outdoor shack, for lack of a better description, that would never make it on the tourist map for any visitor. From the outside, it looks a bit run down and doesn't offer an ambiance that reminds one of a bygone era in any way. But the food is some of the freshest and most plentiful that I've found in Cuba, and you can get a full meal for less than four dollars.

This recipe uses red pepper flakes, olive oil, saffron, and green olives, which you might not find every day in the markets of Havana; however, when added, they bring the flavors of Cuba to life.

Serves 6
INGREDIENTS

4	CLOVES GARLIC, MINCED	½	TSP SAFFRON THREADS
2	TSP RED PEPPER FLAKES	1	RED ONION, CHOPPED
2	TBSP LIME JUICE	3	SMALL BELL PEPPERS, SEEDED AND CHOPPED
½	TSP SALT	1	CAN (15 OZ) DICED TOMATOES
¼	TSP FRESHLY GROUND BLACK PEPPER	1	TSP GROUND CUMIN
2½	LB CHICKEN PIECES, SKIN ON AND BONE IN	2	BAY LEAVES
3	TBSP OLIVE OIL	2	CUPS LONG-GRAIN BROWN RICE
4	CUPS CHICKEN BROTH	1	CUP GREEN OLIVES, HALVED
			CILANTRO, TO GARNISH

PREPARATION

In a large bowl, stir together the garlic, red pepper flakes, lime juice, salt, and pepper. Add the uncooked chicken and toss in the mixture until coated. Once thoroughly coated, refrigerate for at least 1 hour. The longer you marinate the mixture, the more flavorful it will be.

In a large frying pan, heat olive oil over medium heat. Arrange the chicken pieces in the pan, skin side down, and cook until they are golden brown, for about 10 minutes. Flip and repeat on the second side.

In a separate saucepan, warm the broth over medium-high heat. Remove the broth from the heat and sprinkle in saffron, then set aside.

Transfer the marinated chicken to a plate and pour off all but roughly 2 Tbsp of fat from the pan. Add in the onion and bell peppers, and sauté until softened, approximately 3 minutes. Add the tomatoes, cumin, bay leaves, and rice to the pan and cook, stirring constantly, until the rice has absorbed the juices. This will take approximately 5 minutes.

Pour the saffron broth into pan and stir. Place the chicken on top. Raise heat to medium-high and bring to a boil. Reduce heat to low, cover, and simmer for 35 minutes, or until the chicken is cooked through, the rice is starting to get tender, and about half of the liquid has been absorbed.

Remove the lid and cook until the rice is tender, and the liquid has been fully absorbed, about 10 to 15 additional minutes. Stir occasionally to prevent the rice from sticking to the bottom of the pan. Cut into the chicken to be sure that it is cooked through.

Let stand for 5 minutes. Garnish with olives and cilantro.

Chicken and Rice

A simple dish, chicken and rice is a mainstay of Cuban cuisine. The addition of bija, wine, and cumin really bring the dish to life.

INGREDIENTS

2 LB CHICKEN

SALT AND PEPPER, TO TASTE

1½ CUPS RICE

OIL, FOR THE PANS

6 TBSP CHICKEN STOCK

5 DASHES BIJA

1 CLOVE GARLIC, FINELY CHOPPED

1½ ONION, FINELY CHOPPED

⅓ RED BELL PEPPER, FINELY CHOPPED

1 SMALL FRESH TOMATO, FINELY CHOPPED

1 BAY LEAF, CRUSHED

1 TSP CUMIN

1 TSP OF OREGANO, CRUSHED

PARSLEY, MINCED

3 TBSP SWEET RED PEPPER (PIMENTO), SLICED

2 EGGS, HARD BOILED

PEAS

PREPARATION

Clean the chicken and cut into quarters. Season with salt and pepper.

Cook the rice and then lightly fry it in an oiled pan. Set aside for later.

Stir fry the chicken in the pan until browned. Add the chicken stock and bija.

In another pan, heat oil, and add in garlic, onion, pepper, and tomato.

In a clay pot, add in the lightly fried rice with the sauce and broth. Add in the crushed bay leaf, cumin, oregano, and parsley. Let this mixture cook until the grains cook through.

Serve the chicken on a bed of rice and top with pimentos, hard boiled eggs, and peas.

Fricasé de Pollo

CUBAN-STYLE CHICKEN STEW

The flavors from alcaparrado (a mix of pimento-stuffed olives and capers) and sweetness from raisins are what set this dish apart. The perfect cure for your island cold, my first island stew was made by the lovely Vivian, who tends to the house where I regularly stay, after I had a terrible bout of the flu. "Li-zee" is what she calls me, and though we don't speak much of the same language (her Spanish is more colloquially Cuban than I can understand at times), her affection for me, and mine for her, is clear. We have become a family of sorts, and the gift of her deep friendship and caretaking has made a home away from home in Cuba a real possibility.

SERVES 4

INGREDIENTS

¼ CUP FRESH LIME JUICE

¼ CUP FRESH ORANGE JUICE

3 CLOVES GARLIC, LIGHTLY SMASHED

1 CHICKEN (3½–4 LB), QUARTERED (BACKBONE DISCARDED OR SAVED FOR STOCK)

SALT AND PEPPER, TO TASTE

⅓ CUP OLIVE OIL

1 LARGE GREEN BELL PEPPER, STEMMED, SEEDED, AND THINLY SLICED

1 LARGE WHITE ONION, THINLY SLICED

1 CUP DRY WHITE WINE

1 LB RUSSET POTATOES, PEELED AND CUT INTO 1-INCH PIECES

½ CUP JARRED ALCAPARRADO OR ⅓ CUP PIMENTO-STUFFED OLIVES

¼ CUP RAISINS

1 CAN (8 OZ) TOMATO SAUCE

½ CUP WATER

1 CUP FROZEN PEAS, DEFROSTED

SERVE WITH:

RICE

PREPARATION

Combine lime juice, orange juice, garlic, chicken, salt, and pepper in a bowl. Cover and chill for 1 hour or more, to marry the flavors.

Heat oil in a large saucepan over medium-high heat. Remove the chicken from the marinade and pat dry using paper towels; reserve the marinade for later. Cook the chicken, flipping once, until browned, 8–10 minutes, and transfer onto a plate. Add the bell pepper and onion to the pan and cook until soft, 6–8 minutes.

Add wine, scraping up browned bits from the bottom of the pan, until the mixture is reduced by half, 5–7 minutes. Return the chicken to the pan and add the reserved marinade, potatoes, alcaparrado, raisins, tomato sauce, and water; season to taste with ample salt and pepper. Bring to a boil. Reduce heat to medium-low, and cook, covered, until the chicken and potatoes are tender, approximately 45 minutes.

Stir in peas about 30 minutes into the cooking process, and once cooked together, serve over a bed of rice.

Mojo Chicken with Chili Roasted Yams

Mojo is a typical Cuban meat marinade made from olive oil, salt, water, garlic, cumin, citrus, and local peppers. The sauce can vary in spice, depending on the specific pepper used, and is found in many Cuban and Caribbean dishes.

SERVES 2-3
INGREDIENTS

MOJO CHICKEN:

1 LARGE LIME, JUICED AND ZESTED

1 ORANGE, JUICED AND ZESTED

2 TBSP OIL

2 TSP SALT

½ TSP PEPPER

1 TSP GROUND CUMIN

8 GARLIC CLOVES

1 SMALL CHICKEN (4-4½ LB)

1-2 TBSP OLIVE OIL

1 ONION, SLICED INTO ½-INCH-THICK RINGS

2 BELL PEPPERS, SLICED INTO ½-INCH-THICK RINGS

1 CUP WHITE WINE

2 BAY LEAVES

ROASTED YAMS:

2 YAMS, CUT INTO ½-INCH-THICK SLICES

2 TBSP OLIVE OIL

½ TSP SALT

½ TSP CHILI POWDER

½ TSP ALLSPICE

LIME JUICE, TO GARNISH

LIME WEDGE, JUICE AND ZEST TO GARNISH

CILANTRO, TO GARNISH

PREPARATION

Prepare the marinade. Add lime juice (reserve the zest), orange juice (reserve the zest), oil, salt, pepper, cumin, and garlic in a blender, and blend well. Place the chicken and marinade in a large ziplock bag or mixing bowl, and mix well. Let sit at room temperature for 1 hour or more.

Preheat the oven to 425°F.

Prepare the vegetables. In a large pan, heat 1 Tbsp olive oil over medium heat. Add the onion and sauté on medium-high heat until golden brown and tender. Add the peppers, and turn the heat to medium, stirring for 3-4 minutes.

Add the wine, orange and lime zest, and bay leaves. Turn off the heat. Remove the chicken from the marinade and set aside on parchment paper. Pour the marinade into the pan with the onion and peppers, and stir.

Place the chicken breast-side down in the pan to soak up the juice. Place the pan on the lower rack of the oven for 20 minutes. Rotate the chicken and reduce the heat to 400°F, until the inner chicken thigh reaches 165°F (use a meat thermometer). This should take approximately 35–45 minutes.

Once cooked thoroughly, let the chicken rest for 10 minutes before carving.

Roasted yams:

Dice yams and place in a medium bowl, mixing in olive oil, salt, chili powder, and allspice. Place the coated yams on a parchment paper–lined baking sheet and roast at 400°F until tender, approximately 30 minutes. Generously drizzle lime juice over the baked yams before serving.

Slice the chicken and serve over a healthy bed of roasted yams, braised peppers and onions, and pan juices. Top with a squeeze of lime juice, touch of lime zest, and cilantro.

Sino-Cubano

CHINESE FRIED RICE

Cuba's Chinese influence might surprise most; however, the Chinese population has existed in Cuba since 1857 when Cantonese and Hakka workers were brought to the island to work in the vast sugar fields. More than 150,000 Chinese men came from mainland China, Hong Kong, Taiwan, and Macau to work alongside the African slaves already on the island. Although the Chinese weren't necessarily considered "slaves," they worked through ruthless conditions and were treated with the same stringent rules that their slave counterparts endured. Most Chinese workers lived in Cuba on an eight-year contract, and once that contract was finished many stayed on, despite wanting to return home. Naturally, races intermixed, adding even more diversity to the already multicultural Cuban race. According to 2008 statistics from the CIA World Factbook, only 300 of the island's 113,000 Chinese are pure Chinese.

The Barrio Chino de La Habana, or Chinatown of Havana, is considered the oldest Chinese neighborhood in Latin America to date. Restaurants, which are more Cuban and Italian in cuisine than Chinese, flank the streets. However, the Chinese influence in Cuban food can still be seen in dishes like fried rice, spring rolls, and fried wontons found in many restaurants on the island.

SERVES 4–6

INGREDIENTS

- Oil, for frying
- 2 lb large shrimp, peeled, deveined, and butterflied
- 4 lobsters, shells removed
- 4 crabs, shells removed
- 6 eggs
- 1 Tbsp soy sauce
- 2 Tbsp chicken stock or broth
- 1 cup chopped onion
- 1 cup chopped green bell pepper

- 3 cloves garlic, minced
- ½ cup diced carrot
- 4 cups cooked rice
- ½ cup chicken stock or broth mixed with 2 Tbsp soy sauce
- 2 cups diced ham
- ½ cup chopped green onions
- ½ cup frozen green peas

PREPARATION

Coat a frying pan with oil and sauté the shrimp, lobster, and crab, and set aside.

Beat the eggs with a whisk, adding in the soy sauce and chicken broth.

Heat 1 Tbsp oil in a large 5-quart sauté pan, coating the bottom and sides thoroughly. When the oil is sizzling hot, pour half of the egg mixture in so it coats the bottom of the pan. Lower the heat to medium-low and cook the egg through, flipping once. Remove from the pan and cut the egg into strips.

In the same pan sauté the onion and green pepper over medium-low heat until the onion becomes translucent.

Turn the heat down to low. Add the garlic and carrots. Continue to cook for approximately 1–2 minutes, and remove from heat before the garlic browns.

Add the rice and a dash of oil to the pan and fry for approximately 5 minutes, stirring frequently. Add in enough chicken broth to flavor the rice, but not enough to make it soupy. Add in the second half of the egg mixture. Add the ham and cooked seafood, and stir. Continue cooking for approximately 5 minutes.

Fold in the green onions, green peas, and egg strips. Remove from the heat, cover, and let stand for 1–2 minutes.

pescado y marisco

The future of Cuban food must be the sea.
Despite our roots, and the opportunity to travel and know
international food is fundamental to the development
of our own food culture here in Cuba.

—GUSTAVO CARI, OWNER OF RÍO MAR

Paladar Vistamar

The sprawling view of water and fresh seafood are the signature marks of Paladar Vistamar, Miramar's mid-century modern residence that lies between sea and town. The easy feel of dining beside the bay is one that pre-revolutionary Cubans enjoyed quite well.

Vistamar is one of the few renovated houses in the neighborhood (although that is rapidly changing), and it draws an international clientele.

"This restaurant came to be because of my grandmother, Berta Fernandez," owner Alejandro Guerrero told me. "In 1996, when paladares were given licenses to start a private business, the restaurant opened its doors with the intention of creating a new concept, linked to a Brazilian telenovela called 'Vale Todo.' Cubans really liked this telenovela, and because it was the Special Period and people had so little, they stopped everything that they were doing to watch it every day of the week. Watching this telenovela and eating Cuban food was a necessary pleasure of that period. Chefs introduced our recipes, which were mostly international, but adapted to the concept of the paladar."

"The idea has always been to go toward a new cuisine," he continued, while proudly straightening the chairs that line the pool by the restaurant. "Our hope is for a cuisine that is still Cuban but offers a modern twist." The métier specialty of the house is fish, and the seafood salads are praised by clientele, as well. "The house offers something that's special: seafood with a modern Cuban feel . . . it is a fantastic mix."

"Our young family comes from a generation that didn't know fine dining because of the time we grew up in," Guerrero adds. But his grandmother, Berta, who can be found at the helm of the establishment, certainly knew a finer life. Berta Fernandez's elegance and grace seem almost out of place in a country so filled with rubble and decay. When we met, I was reminded of a movie star from a forgotten era—at eighty-some years, Berta had a poised stance, a firm handshake, and a long, elegant floral hostess gown from the 50s. Her hair was coiffed to perfection, and her ears were adorned with pearls.

Berta has managed to maintain the essence of Cuba's upper class, despite her family's many hardships from decades of embargo life, and it is clear when speaking with her grandson that she raised him to know that there was always something more.

"We have worked hard, and now famous chefs from other countries come to visit Vistamar," said Guerrero. "We are always open to suggestions on new and interesting cuisines. That said, it is very difficult sometimes to apply what we learn from others, and it is also difficult to adapt recipes to what we have available in Cuba, but we still manage to provide good service and a tasty dish."

Arroz Amarillo y Camarones

YELLOW RICE AND SHRIMP

Bijol, known as "achiote" or "annatto" powder, is a condiment used to color rice. Saffron is rarely available in Cuba, and Bijol is a common substitute, mainly for the vibrant yellow that it produces. While Bijol tastes different from saffron, it boasts a flavor that Cubans love. Bijol was created by the Bijol Company in Cuba in 1922, from a mixture of corn flour, annatto, and ground cumin. It provides good flavor without the use of MSG and became popular in the United States and the Caribbean in 1942. Today, it can be found outside of Cuba in well-stocked Latin American specialty stores.

SERVES 6
INGREDIENTS

2 LB LARGE SHRIMP, PEELED, DEVEINED, AND BUTTERFLIED (SAVE SHELLS)	3 CUPS CHICKEN BROTH
1 QUART WATER	3 CUPS UNCOOKED RICE
½ TSP SALT	1 CAN (14 OZ) TOMATOES, CHOPPED
¼ CUP OLIVE OIL	1 TSP BIJOL POWDER
2 CUPS DICED WHITE ONION	1½ TSP SALT
1½ CUPS DICED RED BELL PEPPER	¼ TSP PEPPER
1½ CUPS DICED GREEN BELL PEPPER	6 STRIPS BACON, DICED
4 CLOVES GARLIC, CRUSHED AND FINELY CHOPPED	SALT AND PEPPER, TO TASTE
	GROUND CUMIN, TO TASTE
	⅔ CUP FROZEN GREEN PEAS

PREPARATION

Make a broth from the shells of the shrimp by placing them in a 3-quart saucepan along with the water and salt. Bring the pot to a boil, reduce heat to low, and let simmer uncovered for approximately 10 minutes.

In a large sauté pan, add the olive oil and sauté the onion, red pepper, and green pepper until the onion is translucent. Add in garlic and cook for 1–2 minutes, stirring frequently.

Remove the pot of simmering shrimp shells from the heat and strain out the shells and discard. Pour 3 cups of shrimp broth into a large pot and cover with a lid. Add cooked peppers and onions, chicken broth, rice, tomatoes, Bijol, salt, and pepper. Bring the mixture to a boil, then immediately reduce the heat to low, re-cover the pot, and simmer until the rice is cooked and most of the liquid has been absorbed, approximately 30–45 minutes.

As you wait for the rice mixture to cook, sauté bacon in a large frying pan. Reduce the heat to medium-low, and let the fat render out of the bacon, approximately 10 minutes. Once the fat is released, remove the bacon from the pan and raise the temperature to high. Add in peeled shrimp to the steaming hot bacon fat. Season the shrimp lightly with salt, pepper, and a dash of cumin. Sauté the shrimp, flipping once after 1–2 minutes, until they turn pink, approximately 3 minutes.

Remove the shrimp from the pan and set aside, covering them to keep warm. Do not let them continue to cook, though.

Fluff the cooked rice mixture with a fork and add in peas. Gradually fold the cooked shrimp into the cooked rice and heat together for approximately 3 minutes to make sure that the final dish can be served hot.

Arroz con Mariscos

RICE WITH SEAFOOD

One of the many rice dishes common on Cuban menus, arroz con mariscos is a house specialty at seaside eateries like Vistamar and Río Mar.

SERVES 8–10
INGREDIENTS

2 QUARTS WATER	1 TSP BIJOL POWDER
1 TSP SALT	1½ TSP SALT
1 LB LARGE SHRIMP, PEELED, DEVEINED, AND BUTTERFLIED (RESERVE SHELLS)	¼ TSP PEPPER
	6 STRIPS BACON, DICED
2 LOBSTER TAILS (4–6 OZ EACH) (RESERVE SHELLS)	1 LB BAY SCALLOPS
	OLIVE OIL, FOR FRYING (OPTIONAL)
¼ CUP OLIVE OIL	SALT AND PEPPER, TO TASTE
2 CUPS WHITE ONION, DICED	GROUND CUMIN, TO TASTE
1½ CUPS RED BELL PEPPER, DICED	2 TBSP FRESH LEMON JUICE
1½ CUPS GREEN BELL PEPPER, DICED	½ LB FISH FILLETS (OF YOUR CHOICE)
6 CLOVES GARLIC, CRUSHED AND FINELY CHOPPED	¼ CUP FLOUR
	⅔ CUP FROZEN GREEN PEAS
3 CUPS PARBOILED RICE	
1 CUP ROMA TOMATOES, CHOPPED	

Octopus can be substituted for lobster, shrimp, and scallops.

PREPARATION

Fill a large 3-quart saucepan with 2 quarts water and add salt. Add in shells from the shrimp and lobster. Bring the pan to a rapid boil, then reduce the heat to low and let simmer for approximately 15 minutes.

Add olive oil to a large sauté pan and sauté the onion and pepper until the onion is translucent. Add in garlic and cook for 1–2 minutes, stirring frequently. Do not let the garlic brown.

Remove the simmering broth from the heat and strain out the shells and discard. Pour 6 cups of this seafood broth into a large 8-quart covered pot. Add the cooked onion mixture, rice, tomatoes, Bijol powder, salt, and pepper to the broth. Bring this to a boil, then reduce the heat to low, cover, and let simmer until the rice is cooked. Once the majority of the liquid has been absorbed, approximately 30–45 minutes, the rice is ready.

While waiting for the rice to cook, sauté the bacon in a large frying pan. Reduce the heat to medium-low and let the fat render out, approximately 10 minutes. Once the fat releases, remove the bacon and set aside.

Increase the temperature to high, and sauté the shrimp, lobster tails, and scallops in the hot bacon fat, in this order. If needed, add a drizzle or spoonful of olive oil to the pan to keep the bottom moist. Season the seafood with a touch of salt and pepper and a dash of cumin. Sauté the seafood quickly, flipping once after 1–2 minutes, until the shrimp turns pink and the scallops and lobster tails turn opaque, approximately 3 to 5 minutes. Remove the seafood and set aside keeping it warm; do not let it continue to cook.

Drizzle lemon juice on the fish fillets, and lightly season with salt, pepper, and a dash of cumin. Coat the fillets in flour on both sides, and fry in the pan until just cooked through.

Fluff the rice up with a fork and fold the peas, bacon, and cooked seafood into the rice. Cover and cook over low heat for approximately 3 minutes to ensure that everything is hot and the flavors come together.

Camarones en Crema con Cilantro

SHRIMP IN CILANTRO SAUCE

Seafood is reserved for tourists, and a license to fish is as rare as anything on the island. Shrimp can be found on the menu of prominent restaurants.

SERVES 4-6
INGREDIENTS

1 QUART WATER	1 CUP ROMA TOMATOES, SEEDED AND CHOPPED
1 TSP SALT	
2 LB SHRIMP, PEELED AND DEVEINED (RESERVE SHELLS)	4 CLOVES GARLIC, CHOPPED
	SALT AND PEPPER, TO TASTE
½ CUP (1 STICK) SALTED BUTTER	1 CUP HEAVY CREAM
¼ CUP FLOUR	⅓ CUP FRESH CILANTRO, CHOPPED
¼ CUP WHITE WINE	**SERVE WITH:**
¼ CUP OLIVE OIL	RICE
½ CUP CHOPPED ONION	LIME SLICE, TO GARNISH

PREPARATION

Fill a pot with water and add salt. Make a stock by boiling shrimp shells in the lightly salted water. Strain, discarding the shells, and reserve the stock.

Using a 3-quart saucepan, melt the butter over medium-low heat until it just begins to brown. Whisk in the flour quickly to make a smooth roux or paste. Add 1 cup shrimp stock and the wine, blending with your whisk to avoid any lumps. Simmer over low heat, stirring constantly until the sauce thickens. Remove from direct heat, cover, and keep warm for later.

In a large sauté pan over medium heat, add olive oil and sauté the onion until it begins to soften. Add the shrimp and continue to sauté for 1-2 minutes only, flipping frequently. Add the tomatoes and garlic, and cook for an additional 3-5 minutes, stirring occasionally. Salt and pepper to taste.

While the shrimp is cooking, finish your sauce. Add the cream to the roux and use a whisk to blend thoroughly. Return to the medium heat to bring the sauce up to serving temperature. Stir constantly, and do not let the sauce come to a boil. Remove sauce from heat and add the fresh cilantro.

Pour the sauce over the shrimp and vegetables in the sauté pan, mixing with a spoon to blend.

Serve over a bed of rice and garnish with a slice of lime.

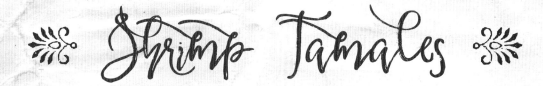

Shrimp Tamales

Cuban tamales are all made with corn, and stuffing varies depending on region. Shrimp tamales are commonly found in high-end restaurants in Havana and along the sea in Trinidad.

SERVINGS: 14–16 TAMALES

INGREDIENTS

SOFRITO SAUCE:

1 MEDIUM ONION, FINELY CHOPPED

1 GREEN BELL PEPPER, STEMMED, SEEDED, AND FINELY CHOPPED

1 CUBANELLE PEPPER, STEMMED, SEEDED, AND FINELY CHOPPED

1 PASILLA PEPPER, STEMMED, SEEDED, AND FINELY CHOPPED

1 TBSP FINELY CHOPPED FRESH OREGANO

1 TSP GROUND CUMIN

1 DRIED MULATO CHILE POD, STEMMED, SEEDED, AND CHOPPED OR TORN INTO TINY PIECES

12 MEDIUM CLOVES GARLIC, FINELY CHOPPED

1 CUP FRESHLY SQUEEZED ORANGE JUICE OR BITTER ORANGE MARINADE (SUCH AS GOYA BRAND)

3 TBSP SPANISH OLIVE OIL

¼ CUP DRY WHITE WINE

TAMALES:

1 PACKAGE (8 OZ) DRIED CORN HUSKS (ABOUT 50 HUSKS)

3 BAGS (1 LB EACH) FROZEN CORN KERNELS, DEFROSTED, COARSELY CHOPPED IN A FOOD PROCESSOR

¾–1 CUP MASA HARINA (FINELY GROUND CORNMEAL)

1 LB SMALL COOKED SHRIMP, PEELED, DEVEINED, AND COARSELY CHOPPED IN A FOOD PROCESSOR

SALT AND FRESHLY GROUND BLACK PEPPER, TO TASTE

PREPARATION

Prepare the sofrito first, by combining the onion, green bell pepper, cubanelle pepper, pasilla pepper, oregano, cumin, dried mulato chili, garlic, and orange juice or bitter orange marinade in a large mixing bowl.

Add olive oil to a large skillet. Cook the onion mixture in the skillet over medium-high heat for approximately 15 minutes, stirring occasionally, until the liquid has evaporated and the mixture seems almost dry. Add the wine (including a sip for you), and cook for approximately 3–4 minutes until the wine evaporates.

Prepare the tamales. Soak the corn husks in warm water for 1 hour. Each tamale requires 3 husks, but they can break during the process, so soak a few extra.

Place the coarsely processed corn in a large saucepan over medium-low to medium heat. Cook for 5 minutes until the corn is thoroughly warmed through. Gradually add the masa harina (as needed), stirring constantly to create a thickened mixture that holds together and pulls away from the sides of the pan, approximately 5 minutes; adjust the heat as needed.

Stir the sofrito mixture into the corn mixture, then gently add in the shrimp. Salt and pepper to taste, making sure that the mixture is salty, as the tamales will lose flavor as they cook. Transfer the mixture to a large bowl. Cover and refrigerate for 20–30 minutes until cool enough to handle.

Assemble the tamales: bring a large stockpot of water to a boil over high heat. Drain and pat dry the soaked corn husks on a clean, dry towel. Cut 14–16 lengths of kitchen twine, about 16 inches each, to tie the tamales later.

Work on a clean, dry surface. Align 2 corn husks and overlap the sides. Top with ⅓–½ cup of the shrimp-corn mixture and fold in the long sides of the corn husks so the filling is completely covered. Fold in the top and bottom ends, to make an envelope-like package. Tie the tamale with kitchen twine (horizontally, at the center) to secure the stuffing. Continue the process to create 14–16 tamales.

Reduce the heat under the boiling water to medium, and add the tamales. Cook for 45 minutes, making sure the water never returns to a rolling boil. Transfer to a colander to drain, and cool slightly before unwrapping. The tamales' filling will be soft and should pull away slightly from the husks. Serve warm.

Empanadas Decameron

SHRIMP EMPANADAS

The most flavorful empanadas that I've tasted in Cuba are made by the kitchen of Cuba's notable restaurant, Decameron. Despite the small kitchen and typically well-worn 1950s cooking equipment, including decades-old pots and pans, Decameron has an ambiance and menu that are among the best on the island. Inspired by the cuisine of Italy, the restaurant creates light pastas, fresh homemade breads, and refreshing salads.

SERVINGS: 24 EMPANADAS

INGREDIENTS

SHRIMP FILLING:

- ¼ CUP OLIVE OIL
- 1 CUP SWEET ONION, DICED SMALL
- 2 TBSP GARLIC, MINCED
- 2½ CUPS TOMATOES, DICED INTO MEDIUM-SIZE CUBES
- 2½ TBSP CUMIN POWDER
- 2 TSP ANCHO CHILI POWDER
- ¾ CUP CILANTRO, ROUGHLY CHOPPED
- 26–30 SHRIMP (2½ LB), CLEANED AND CHOPPED
- SALT AND PEPPER, TO TASTE

HONEY PICANTE SAUCE:

- 1 CUP SALSA PICANTE (HOT SAUCE)
- 1 CUP HONEY
- 2 JALAPEÑOS, STEMMED AND SEEDED
- ½ CUP CILANTRO, ROUGHLY CHOPPED
- 1 OZ WHITE VINEGAR
- 1 TSP CRUSHED RED PEPPER
- JUICE OF 1 LIME

- 36 4-INCH DISCOS (ROUND DOUGH SHELLS), HOMEMADE OR COMMERCIALLY PREPARED
- OIL, FOR DEEP FRYING

PREPARATION

Prepare the shrimp filling first. In a large sauté pan, add olive oil, onions, and garlic. Once the mixture softens, add in the tomatoes, cumin, and chili powder, and cook for several minutes. Add in cilantro and the chopped shrimp, simmering for 3-4 minutes until the shrimp are lightly cooked through. Salt and pepper to taste. Remove from heat and chill.

Prepare the honey picante sauce. Puree all sauce ingredients in a blender.

Lay out the empanada dough shells on a clean work surface. Place a substantial dollop of filling in the center of each piece of dough. Fold the dough over and crimp the sides with a fork or your fingers. Deep fry in oil at 350°F until golden brown.

Serve with honey picante sauce on the side for dipping.

Enchilado de Langosta y Camarones

SPICY LOBSTER AND SHRIMP STEW

Fresh, succulent, meaty lobster is ideal for this dish. Try using Maine lobster when available as a good alternative to the Cuban variety.

SERVES 10-12

INGREDIENTS

6–8 SPINY LOBSTER TAILS

½ CUP OLIVE OIL

1–2 LB SHRIMP, PEELED, DEVEINED, AND DE-TAILED

½ CUP WHITE WINE

1 TBSP WHITE WINE VINEGAR

2 LARGE ONIONS, FINELY CHOPPED

4–6 GARLIC CLOVES, MINCED

1 LARGE RED SWEET PEPPER, FINELY CHOPPED

1 BAY LEAF

1 CAN (6 OZ) TOMATO PASTE

1 CAN (15 OZ) CRUSHED TOMATOES

¾ CUP RED ENCHILADA SAUCE

1 BUNCH ITALIAN PARSLEY, FINELY CHOPPED

1 SMALL CAN PIMENTOS, MINCED (OPTIONAL)

SALT AND PEPPER, TO TASTE

SERVE WITH:

RICE AND BAGUETTES

PREPARATION

Using a large knife for chopping, cut the fresh lobster tails into 3 sections. Heat a large pot over medium heat, and add olive oil to the pan. Once the oil is hot, add the lobster rings and shrimp and sauté. Add the white wine and white wine vinegar until the shrimp and lobster become opaque, approximately 5 minutes. Remove with a slotted spoon and set aside.

Sauté the onions, garlic, red pepper, and bay leaf in the remaining oil for about 10 minutes, or until the onions are completely translucent and soft. Stir in the tomato paste, crushed tomatoes, enchilada sauce, parsley, and pimientos (optional). Bring to a steady simmer, about 15 minutes. Add salt and pepper to taste.

Return the cooked seafood to the pot and let simmer uncovered for 15–20 minutes, making sure the seafood does not toughen.

Serve immediately with rice and a baguette to enjoy the sauce.

Like most things in Cuba, the complicated story of lobster is a result of the ever-changing political system. At the moment, lobster is expressly reserved for tourists and for export, and restaurants typically procure lobster through the black market. Fishermen are required to have a license, and very few licenses are given out. Cubans are forbidden from going on boats, and the demand from tourists who expect lobster in the tropical island's cuisine forces the black market to fill in the gaps for many successful paladares. The "don't ask, don't tell" theory seems to be consistently applied to these black markets, but individual families who could benefit from the fruits of the sea are left wanting as the tourist demand depletes the market. "Lobster pirates" are stopped by police on the highway and given fines of up to CUC$2000, which is more than a year's salary for most Cubans, making the illegal lobster trade even more dangerous and secretive.

Mojito Ceviche

The mojito, a favorite cocktail of Ernest Hemingway, plays such a large part in the ambiance of Havana. La Bodeguita del Medio, the bar that claims the creation of the drink, is swarmed by tourists lining up along the streets waiting for a glass. If you go, bring a pen and add your name to the graffitied wall alongside some of the bar's most famed visitors. The mojito's five main ingredients (white rum, sugar, lime juice, soda water, and mint) are a perfect marinade for chicken or fish.

SERVES 4
INGREDIENTS

CEVICHE:

¾ LB SEMI-FIRM WHITE FISH AND/OR SHELLFISH (SEA BASS, TILAPIA, COBIA, SHRIMP, OR SCALLOPS), DICED INTO ¼ INCH CUBES, SHRIMP CUT IN HALF

4 LIMES, ZESTED AND JUICED (ABOUT ½ CUP LIME JUICE)

1 TBSP CLUB SODA

1 TSP SUGAR

½ TSP SEA SALT

¼ TSP PEPPER

1 TBSP WHITE RUM

1 LARGE CLOVE GARLIC, MINCED

⅓ ONION, DICED OR JULIENNED (ABOUT ½ CUP)

1 LARGE JALAPEÑO, RIBS AND SEEDS REMOVED PARTIALLY OR FULLY, MINCED

2 ROMA OR PLUM TOMATOES, SEEDED AND DICED (ABOUT ¾ CUP)

¼ CUP CHOPPED MINT

2 TBSP SNIPPED CHIVES

SEASONING:

SALT AND PEPPER, TO TASTE

LIME JUICE, TO TASTE

MINT, TO GARNISH

LIME WEDGES, TO GARNISH

PREPARATION

Place the cubed raw fish and/or shellfish in a medium-size mixing bowl. Add the lime juice (reserve the zest for later), club soda, sugar, salt, pepper, and rum. Evenly coat the fish. Cover and refrigerate for at least 30–40 minutes to allow the fish to partially "cook." Gently stir the ceviche every 10 minutes to evenly marinate the fish.

When the fish is close to being "cooked through" (it turns opaque), add the rest of the ceviche ingredients and gently toss them in to combine flavors. Taste, adjust the seasoning by adding more of whatever is needed, re-cover the bowl, and return to the refrigerator for another 10 minutes to allow all the flavors to marry.

Remove the ceviche from the refrigerator. Taste and season with salt, pepper, and lime juice. Garnish with mint and lime wedges.

Pescao En Escabeche

FISH WITH ESCABECHE SAUCE

Common in local cafeterias (street restaurants frequented by locals), this white fish dish—served in cazuelas, or earthenware dishes—is topped with an olive-oil-and-vinegar pickling sauce.

SERVES 6
INGREDIENTS

6 SWORDFISH STEAKS (8 OZ EACH), CUT ½-INCH THICK

12 CLOVES GARLIC, MINCED; DIVIDED

KOSHER SALT AND FRESHLY GROUND BLACK PEPPER, TO TASTE

2 CUPS FLOUR

1 CUP EXTRA-VIRGIN OLIVE OIL

4 BAY LEAVES

2 LARGE GREEN BELL PEPPERS, STEMMED, SEEDED, AND CUT INTO ¼-INCH-THICK RINGS

1 LARGE YELLOW ONION, CUT INTO ¼-INCH-THICK RINGS

2 CUPS DISTILLED WHITE VINEGAR

SERVE WITH:

RICE

PREPARATION

Rub the steaks with half the garlic, and thoroughly season with salt and pepper on both sides. Let sit for 20 minutes.

Place flour in a shallow plate, and coat each fish steak, shaking to remove excess flour.

Heat oil in a skillet over medium-high heat until sizzling. Add fish steaks and cook, turning over once, until browned on both sides and cooked through, approximately 5 minutes. Transfer the fish steaks to a serving bowl, and set aside.

Add the remaining garlic to the oil and cook, until golden brown, approximately 1 minute. Add in the bay leaves, peppers, and onion, and cook, until softened, approximately 4 minutes. Add in the vinegar and bring to a boil.

Pour the sauce over the fish steaks and let sit at room temperature for 1 hour before serving with a bed of rice.

Seafood Creole

This dish combines the flavors of the sea with a zesty Creole influence, brought to Cuba at the start of the nineteenth century.

SERVES 4

INGREDIENTS

4 TBSP butter	¼ TSP freshly ground black pepper
1 medium green pepper, chopped	Olive oil, for sautéing
1 large onion, chopped	2 links chorizo, diced
1 cup chopped celery	1 lb shrimp, peeled and deveined
5 cloves garlic, minced	1 lb scallops
6 medium, ripe Roma tomatoes, peeled and chopped	4 lobster tails, shell on, chopped in quarters
¼ cup water	8 mussels
¼ cup tomato juice	Salt and pepper, to taste
1 TBSP lemon juice	¼ cup chopped fresh cilantro
2 TSP cumin	Lime juice, to garnish
2 cups white wine, divided	**SERVE WITH:**
½ TSP salt	Arroz moro

PREPARATION

Add butter, green pepper, onion, and celery to a large sauce pan and place on medium heat. Sauté until the onion is translucent and the celery softens. Add in garlic and sauté for 1-2 minutes.

Add tomatoes, water, tomato juice, lemon juice, cumin, ¼ cup white wine, salt, and pepper to the mix, and bring to a boil. Once at full boil, reduce heat and let simmer, uncovered, for approximately 15 minutes.

As the mix simmers, add enough olive oil to cover the base of a frying pan. Fry the chorizo until the oil turns orange. Remove the chorizo and set aside; reserve the oil. Add in the shrimp, scallops, and lobster tails, and sauté until the shrimp is bright, the lobster tail pink, and the scallops firm and white.

Using the remaining 1¾ cups white wine, steam the mussels in a pan. The wine should just cover the base of the pan. Steam on high heat until the mussels just open.

Add the seafood to the pan of vegetables and sauce. Stir and season with salt and pepper to taste. Simmer the mixture for an additional 2-3 minutes to marry the flavors.

Remove from the heat, sprinkle with fresh cilantro and a squeeze of lime juice, and serve over a bed of arroz moro.

Huevos

Baked Eggs With Sofrito

Eggs are a staple of every Cuban household and are easy to come by. Carried from the shop open-air on exposed egg crates, the precarious storage and transportation of eggs is a testament to the agility with which Cubans move. I have yet to see a flat of raw eggs dropped on the cracked and pock-filled streets and have tasted many an egg for breakfast on the island.

SERVES 4
INGREDIENTS

SOFRITO:

4 PLUM TOMATOES

1 JALAPEÑO PEPPER, STEM REMOVED

OLIVE OIL, TO COAT THE BAKING SHEET

½ ONION, SLICED

2 GARLIC CLOVES

1 TBSP FRESH CILANTRO

PINCH OF FINE GRAIN SEA SALT, TO TASTE

PINCH OF GROUND CUMIN

4 CORN TORTILLAS

4 ORGANIC EGGS

FINE GRAIN SEA SALT AND PEPPER, TO TASTE

1 AVOCADO, PITTED AND SLICED

1 BUNCH CILANTRO, WASHED AND STEMMED

ANCHO CHILE POWDER, TO TASTE

PREPARATION

Prepare the sofrito first. Preheat your oven to broil. Line two small baking sheets with aluminum foil. Place the tomatoes and jalapeño on one baking sheet and broil for about 5-7 minutes. Flip the tomatoes and jalapeño over and broil for another 5-7 minutes until the jalapeño skins are charred and the tomatoes are split open. Remove them from the oven and let cool until they are warm.

Turn the oven temperature down to 400°F. Lightly coat the foil-lined baking sheets with olive oil, add the onion and garlic, and bake for about 15-20 minutes until the onion edges are charred and the garlic is soft. Remove from the oven and let cool slightly.

Peel and core the broiled tomatoes, and add in a food processor. Cut the broiled jalapeño into 3 pieces and add 1 piece in the processor. Add garlic and onion, and blend in the food processor. Add in the cilantro, salt, and cumin. Mix until pureed, then refrigerate the mixture until you are ready to use.

Prepare the eggs. Preheat your oven to 350°F. Place the tortillas inside four ramekins, and crack an egg into each tortilla-lined ramekin. Sprinkle with salt and pepper and place the ramekins on a baking sheet in the oven. Bake until the whites of the eggs are firm, approximately 15-20 minutes, rotating the ramekins halfway through.

Remove the ramekins from the oven and top the dish with sofrito, avocado, cilantro, the remaining jalapeño (sliced), and a dash of ancho chile powder.

Huevos a la Flamenco

FLAMENCO-STYLE EGGS

Creamy eggs with savory Spanish chorizo. The Spanish came to Cuba in 1492, when Christopher Columbus landed on the island. Today, much of the Spanish colonial culture remains, and food has certainly been influenced by Spanish roots.

SERVES 4

INGREDIENTS

2	TBSP OLIVE OIL, PLUS EXTRA
1	MEDIUM ONION, CHOPPED
3	CLOVES GARLIC, MASHED
½	CUP GREEN PEAS
½	CUP GARBANZO BEANS
½	CUP DICED CARROTS
¼	CUP TOMATO SAUCE

SALT AND PEPPER, TO TASTE

4 SLICES HAM

4 CHORIZO SAUSAGE LINKS, SLICED

8 EGGS

SERVE WITH:

TOAST AND FRESH MANGO JUICE

PREPARATION

Preheat oven to 375°F.

Add 2 Tbsp olive oil to a pan over medium heat. Sauté the onion until translucent. Add the garlic, peas, garbanzo beans, and carrots. Add the tomato sauce and simmer on low for 15 minutes. Salt and pepper to taste.

Lightly oil four custard cups and add a healthy portion of the vegetable mixture in each. Top with one slice of ham and slices of chorizo. Crack 2 eggs into each dish, and allow the eggs to float on top.

Place the dishes in the oven and bake for 15–20 minutes, or until the egg whites turn white. The yolks should be slightly runny.

Serve with a side of toast and fresh mango juice.

Huevos Enchilados

EGGS POACHED IN SOFRITO SAUCE

Delicate poached eggs with savory sofrito. Sofrito is one of the most common sauces in Cuba. Similar to roux, made with flour and found in Creole cuisine, this sauce combines tomatoes, garlic, green bell pepper, onions, and sometimes chorizo.

SERVES 4
INGREDIENTS

SOFRITO:

2 TBSP OLIVE OIL

1 CUP CHOPPED ONION

2 CUPS CORED AND CHOPPED RED AND GREEN BELL PEPPER

3 CLOVES GARLIC, MASHED

3 TBSP WHITE WINE

1 CUP PEELED, CORED, AND CHOPPED FRESH TOMATO

1 CAN (14.5 OZ) TOMATO SAUCE

1 TSP GROUND CUMIN

½ TSP SALT

¼ TSP PEPPER

8 EGGS

SEASONING:

PAPRIKA, TO TASTE

AVOCADO, PITTED AND SLICED

LIME JUICE, TO TASTE

DOLLOP OF SOUR CREAM

CILANTRO LEAVES, TO GARNISH

PREPARATION

Preheat oven to 250°F.

Prepare the sofrito. Add olive oil to a pan over low heat. Sauté the onion and red and green bell peppers until translucent. Add the garlic, and cook just 1-2 minutes more, stirring occasionally.

Pour in wine, tomatoes, tomato sauce, and the cumin. Cook over low heat for approximately 5 minutes, stirring frequently. Add salt and pepper.

Bring the mixture to a near boil, then crack the eggs, one at a time, into a small ramekin. Carefully pour the egg from the ramekin into the hot vegetable mixture so it floats on top. You should be able to cook 4 eggs at a time in a large pan. Cover the pan and cook for approximately 3-4 minutes more, until the eggs are fully cooked and solidified. Scoop out the 4 poached eggs with half of the sofrito mixture, and cook the remaining 4 eggs in the other half of the mixture.

To serve, scoop the sofrito, along with 2 poached eggs per serving, into individual serving bowls. For added zing, lightly dust the top of the eggs with paprika, garnish with a generous slice of fresh avocado, sprinkle a drizzling of lime juice, and add a heaping spoon of sour cream. Finish with a few cilantro leaves.

Tortilla Española de Mar

SEAFOOD SPANISH OMELET

The island of Cuba has deep Spanish influence dating back to the arrival of Christopher Columbus in 1492, when Cuba became a Spanish colony. This dish can be made without seafood for a delicious vegetarian version.

SERVES 4-6
INGREDIENTS

1 CUP PEELED AND THINLY SLICED NEW POTATOES

WATER, TO PARBOIL POTATOES

SALT, FOR THE WATER

OLIVE OIL, FOR SAUTÉING

1 CUP CHOPPED ONION

SALT AND PEPPER, TO TASTE

CUMIN, TO TASTE

1 LB MEDIUM SHRIMP, PEELED AND DEVEINED

2 LOBSTER TAILS (4-6 OZ EACH), MEAT REMOVED FROM SHELL AND CUT IN BITE-SIZE PIECES

½ LB COOKED CRABMEAT

12 EGGS

SALT AND PEPPER, TO TASTE

5 TBSP SOFT BUTTER, ROOM TEMPERATURE

CHOPPED PARSLEY, TO GARNISH

PREPARATION

Parboil the potatoes by placing them in a saucepan full of water, lightly salted. Bring to a boil, reduce heat to low, and simmer until potatoes are tender, approximately 15-20 minutes. Drain out the water.

Add enough olive oil to a pan to coat the bottom. Sauté the parboiled potatoes with the onions until lightly browned; stir frequently to avoid burning. Season the potatoes and onions with salt, pepper, and cumin. Remove the potatoes and onions from the pan and set aside.

Add a dash of oil to the pan. Sauté the shrimp, lobster tails, and crabmeat in small batches until just barely cooked through. They will go from translucent to white, 1-2 minutes. Lightly salt and pepper the seafood as you cook it, turning frequently. It is better to undercook the shrimp and lobster a bit than overcook it. Remove seafood from the pan, and set aside.

In a bowl, beat the eggs with a wire whisk. Add in butter to the eggs and whisk vigorously. Add the cooked potatoes, onions, shrimp, lobster, and crabmeat to the uncooked beaten egg mixture. Salt and pepper to taste.

Heat more olive oil in the pan on medium heat and pour the egg mixture in. Immediately reduce the heat to low and cook for approximately 7-10 minutes. The eggs will become firm and lightly browned.

Cover the pan with a large plate and flip the firm egg mixture over on its other side. Cut the egg tortilla into equal wedges, and garnish with chopped parsley.

Spanish-Cuban Omelet with Chorizo and Savory Potatoes

This dish combines the flavors of the tortilla Española (Spanish omelet) with the light, thin airiness of an American omelet atop a bed of greens. Every table in Cuba has the requisite oil and vinegar, salt, and pepper. While most Cubans do not like the taste of pepper at all, and rarely use it for their own meals, they always have a shaker available for visiting guests.

SERVES 4
INGREDIENTS

1   CUP THINLY SLICED NEW POTATOES

WATER, TO PARBOIL POTATOES

SALT, FOR THE WATER

¼   CUP OLIVE OIL

1   CUP CHOPPED ONION

SALT AND PEPPER, TO TASTE

1   LB CHORIZO, SLICED IN ROUNDS

12   EGGS

5   TBSP SOFT BUTTER, ROOM TEMPERATURE

1   CUP SOUR CREAM

¼   CUP MILK

1   CUP SHREDDED JACK CHEESE

4   TBSP BUTTER

RED WINE VINAIGRETTE DRESSING:

½   CUP RED WINE VINEGAR

1   CUP OLIVE OIL

3   TBSP SUGAR

2   TSP SALT

BLACK PEPPER, TO TASTE

6   CUPS MIXED GREENS

PREPARATION

Parboil the potatoes by placing them in a saucepan full of water, lightly salted. Bring to a boil, reduce heat to low, and simmer until potatoes are tender, approximately 15-20 minutes. Drain out the water.

Heat olive oil in the pan, and sauté the cooked potatoes and onions until they are lightly browned. Stir frequently while seasoning the potatoes and onions with salt and pepper.

Add sliced chorizo to the pan and sauté briefly until heated through. Set the pan aside.

Create the omelet mixture. In a separate bowl, beat the 12 eggs with 5 Tbsp soft butter, and add pinch of salt and dash of pepper. Mix the sour cream and milk, and add to the egg mixture. Sprinkle in the Jack cheese.

Lightly coat the bottom of a skillet with 4 Tbsp butter on low to medium heat. When the butter is melted, pour in the omelet mixture. When the eggs start to cook, add in the chorizo and sautéed vegetables, and fold in half. Flip to cook the other side.

Prepare the red wine vinaigrette dressing. Lightly mix the red wine vinegar, olive oil, sugar, salt, and pepper. Pour over mixed greens, and serve on the side.

Vegetariano

Arroz con Garbanzos

RICE WITH GARBANZO BEANS

The paprika and Bijol make the dish, adding a touch of spice without overwhelming the sweetness of the peppers.

SERVES 6-8

INGREDIENTS

1	LB GARBANZO BEANS, CLEANED AND RINSED	½	TSP BIJOL POWDER
1-2	TBSP OLIVE OIL	3	CUPS CHICKEN BROTH
¼	CUP OLIVE OIL	½	CUP WHITE WINE
2	CUPS DICED ONIONS	½	CUP TOMATO PUREE
1	CUP DICED RED BELL PEPPER	1	TSP SWEET SPANISH PAPRIKA
1	CUP DICED GREEN BELL PEPPER	1	TSP SALT
6	CLOVES GARLIC, MASHED	¼	TSP BLACK PEPPER
1	LINK SPANISH CHORIZO, SLICED	1	CUP DICED ROMA TOMATOES
2	CUPS PARBOILED RICE		

SERVE WITH:

ANY CUBAN MAIN COURSE

PREPARATION

Soak the beans in a large pot filled with water overnight. In the morning, drain the beans and rinse them with fresh water. Put them to a pot of cold water, and add in a 1-2 Tbsp olive oil.

Bring the beans to a boil over high heat, then reduce heat to medium-low, and simmer for 40-60 minutes, or until the beans are cooked and soft.

Add ¼ cup olive oil to a pan over low heat. Sauté the onions and red and green peppers until the onions are translucent. Add in garlic and the chorizo, and cook for 1-2 additional minutes, stirring from time to time to prevent the bottom from burning. This is your sofrito.

In a large saucepan, add the sofrito, garbanzo beans, rice, Bijol powder, chicken broth, wine, tomato puree, paprika, salt, and pepper. Bring the pan to a boil over high heat and cook, uncovered, for 2-3 minutes. Then, cover the pan, reduce heat to low, and let the mixture simmer for approximately 20-30 minutes until the rice is fully cooked.

Fluff the cooked rice with a fork, add in the tomatoes, and serve hot as a side dish to your Cuban main course.

Batido De Mamey

MAMEY SMOOTHIE

A favorite Cuban fruit is the mamey sapote. Mamey's soaplike inner texture and floral flavor lends itself to a number of recipes. The best mamey on the island is grown in the countryside near Trinidad, and local producers wait patiently along the road to sell to customers who are driving by.

INGREDIENTS

1 PACKET (14 OZ) FROZEN MAMEY PULP (GOYA MAKES A GOOD ONE)

1 CUP MILK

½ CUP VANILLA ICE CREAM

ABOUT 1 CUP ICE CUBES

¼–½ CUP SUGAR, ADD TO TASTE

½ TSP VANILLA EXTRACT

PINEAPPLE SLICE, STRAWBERRY, OR LIME SLICE, TO GARNISH

PREPARATION

Combine ingredients in a blender. Puree for 1-2 minutes until a froth forms. Garnish with a slice of pineapple, a fresh strawberry, or a slice of lime.

Bruschetta Cubano

Italian food is more common in Cuba than any other international cuisine. Even at non-Italian restaurants, you'll often find bruschetta on the menu. Tomatoes are abundant on the island, and bread and garlic are easy to come by, as well.

INGREDIENTS

TOPPING:

3 RIPE, BUT FIRM, ROMA TOMATOES, CHOPPED

½ CUP FINELY CHOPPED SWEET ONION

¼ CUP OLIVE OIL

2 TBSP VINEGAR

1 TSP GROUND CUMIN

5 CLOVES GARLIC, MINCED

SALT AND PEPPER, TO TASTE

TOAST:

12 SLICES SOFT FRENCH BREAD

3 CLOVES GARLIC, FINELY MINCED

1 STICK BUTTER, SOFTENED, ROOM TEMPERATURE

¼ CUP CHOPPED CILANTRO

SEA SALT, TO TASTE

PREPARATION

Prepare the topping. Mix the tomatoes, onion, olive oil, vinegar, cumin, and garlic together in a large bowl. Salt and pepper to taste. Cover and refrigerate for 30 minutes or more to let the flavors blend together.

Prepare the toast. Slice the bread into ¾-inch-thick slices. Mix the garlic into the softened butter.

Compress each slice of the bread with a spatula. Butter both sides of the smashed bread with garlic butter. Fry up slices of buttered bread in a frying pan, over medium heat, until lightly toasted on each side.

Spoon the tomato and onion mixture on each slice of toasted bread. Sprinkle the top with chopped cilantro and a touch of sea salt.

Buñuelos con Almíbar

YUCA FRITTERS WITH SYRUP

A popular Cuban dish that's served as a dessert or an appetizer. To find roots and tubers like boniato, malanga, and calabaza, look for them in Caribbean or Cuban specialty markets.

SERVING: 12–14 BUÑUELOS

INGREDIENTS

½ LB YUCA, PEELED AND CUT INTO 1-INCH CHUNKS

¼ LB BONIATO OR SWEET POTATO, PEELED AND CUT INTO 1-INCH CHUNKS

¼ LB MALANGA, PEELED AND CUT INTO 1-INCH CHUNKS

¼ LB ÑAME, PEELED AND CUT INTO 1-INCH CHUNKS

1 TBSP KOSHER SALT

WATER, TO COVER THE VEGETABLES

¼ LB CALABAZA OR OTHER PUMPKIN, PEELED AND CUT INTO 2-INCH CHUNKS

3–4 CUPS UNBLEACHED ALL-PURPOSE FLOUR, PLUS EXTRA

3 LARGE EGGS, WELL BEATEN

2 CUPS CANOLA OIL OR GRAPESEED OIL

SYRUP:

2 CUPS WATER

1 CUP SUGAR

1 WHOLE CINNAMON STICK

3-INCH STRIP LIME ZEST

1–2 TBSP LIME JUICE, FRESHLY SQUEEZED

Boniatos are a flavor cross between a sweet potato and a russet potato. You can find them throughout Florida and the Caribbean and Latin America.

Malanga, also known as yautía, malanga, tannia, tannier, tanier, and cocoyam, has a nutty, earthy, starchy flavor.

Calabaza is a West Indian pumpkin variety with a smooth, sweet flavor that is used in everything from stews to cakes and even candies.

PREPARATION

Combine the yuca, boniato, malanga, ñame, and salt in a heavy pot and cover with cold water.

Bring the water to a boil, lower the heat to medium, and simmer, covered, for 10 minutes.

Add the calabaza and simmer until all the vegetables are tender. Strain water from the pot.

Grind the vegetables in a small food processor and place onto a lightly-floured surface while they are still warm. Mold the pureed vegetables into a mound and form a deep indention in the center that you can pour the beaten eggs into while kneading into the vegetables. Sift 3-4 cups flour over the mixture and combine slowly with your hands until a smooth dough forms. Cut the dough into pieces and roll each piece into strips about ½ inch thick (about the length and width of a french fry).

Heat the oil over medium-high heat in a 10-inch skillet to 375°F. Working in batches, fry the buñuelos until they are golden brown and crispy on each side, approximately 3-4 minutes. Once golden, transfer to a plate lined with paper towels to drain.

Prepare the syrup. Combine all the ingredients except for the lime juice in a saucepan, and bring to a boil. Simmer the mixture. Once it reaches a syrup-like consistency, approximately 15-20 minutes, squeeze in lime juice.

Serve the piping hot syrup with the warm, fried buñuelos.

Campesino Salad

Another throwback to the 1950s, this mayonnaise-based salad is a Cuban party favorite.

INGREDIENTS

1 POTATO, PEELED AND COOKED

2 CARROTS, PEELED

¼ CUP PIMENTOS

2 TOMATOES, STEWED AND COOKED

4 OZ BELL PEPPERS, SLICED

8 EGGS

2 TSP MAYONNAISE

SALT AND PEPPER, TO TASTE

PARSLEY, TO GARNISH

PREPARATION

Cut potatoes, carrots, pimentos, tomatoes, and bell peppers into thin strips, about ½ inch thick. Boil the eggs and peel off the shells. Cut the eggs into quarter slices.

Add the mayonnaise, and mix all the ingredients together in a salad bowl. Salt and pepper to taste, and garnish with a sprig of parsley. Refrigerate for 30 minutes before serving.

Fried Sweet Plantains

Sweet plantains, or plátanos, are a traditional side dish found on every table. The best plantains to use for the dish are overripe fruit with a blackened peel. The darker the peel, the higher the sugar content in the fruit, which yields a sweet flavor and a soft and gooey texture; the charred black edges will also become caramelized and crisp.

Plantains, similar to bananas but with less sugar, are readily accessible—markets in Cuba always have a plentiful supply. In the city, produce sellers will wheel carts to busy corners, and people come from their apartments to purchase needed items for the week.

Green plátanos ripen at room temperature after a few days when placed out of direct sunlight. As the green color of plantains turns to yellow, the starch in the fruit turns to sugar. The next stage of ripeness is when the skin is mostly yellow with a few black speckles. In this stage of ripeness, the plátano has lost some of its starch and is slightly sweet.

SERVES 4

INGREDIENTS

2-3 RIPE PLANTAINS
4 TBSP CANOLA OIL

SALT
POWDERED SUGAR

PREPARATION

Peel the plantains, chop off the ends, slice down the middle, and remove peel. Slice the plantain at an angle into thick wedges.

Heat oil in a large frying pan, and place over medium heat. Add sliced plantains into the oil and cook on both sides until golden brown. The longer you fry the slices, the darker and sweeter they will become.

Remove from heat, and drain on a paper towel. Sprinkle with salt, dust with powdered sugar, and serve hot.

Garlic Mojo Sauce

This sauce or marinade is one of the most common flavors in Cuban cuisine, and it is tasty with meat or fish or any sort. You can easily make this any time with your stocked Cuban pantry.

SERVING: ABOUT 1½ CUPS

INGREDIENTS

½ CUP OLIVE OIL

8 GARLIC CLOVES, PRESSED OR FINELY CHOPPED

1 TSP GROUND CUMIN

½ TSP DRIED OREGANO

1 MEDIUM CHILI POD, THINLY SLICED

½ CUP FRESH LIME JUICE (FROM ABOUT 4 LIMES)

½ CUP FRESH ORANGE JUICE (FROM ABOUT 1 ORANGE)

1½ TSP KOSHER SALT

PREPARATION

Add olive oil to a small saucepan over medium heat. Sauté garlic, cumin, and oregano and cook until tender, then immediately remove from the burner. Let cool for 10-15 minutes.

Stir in the chili, lime juice, orange juice, and salt.

Mango Avocado Salad

Unlike Mexico's abundance of avocados, avocados in Cuba are a rarity. Difficult to find in local markets, avocados typically cost almost as much as a laborer's day's wage. Therefore, when an avocado comes your way in Cuba, you covet it and share with friends.

INGREDIENTS

DRESSING:

¼ CUP OLIVE OIL

3 LIMES, JUICED (ABOUT ¼ CUP)

SPRIG OF CILANTRO

1 TBSP ACHIOTE

2 CLOVES GARLIC

2 TBSP SALT

1 RED BELL PEPPER

½ LARGE SWEET RED ONION, SLICED

2 RIPE AVOCADOS, SLICED

SEA SALT, TO TASTE

½ FRESH MANGO, CUBED

FRESH CILANTRO, CHOPPED

PREPARATION

Prepare the dressing. Whisk olive oil, lime juice, cilantro, achiote, garlic, and salt.

Blanch the bell pepper, and then dice into pieces. Place in a bowl and let cool. Add the dressing to the cooled bell pepper.

Arrange red onion slices on a plate, and top with sliced avocados and a touch of sea salt. Pour dressing over, and top with mango cubes and fresh cilantro.

Malanga Fritters

Similar to yuca fritters, malanga fritters are an island favorite and are served as appetizers and even dessert. Although malanga looks like yam, it has the flavor of a potato.

INGREDIENTS

8½ oz malanga
1 clove garlic, minced
2 eggs
2 Tbsp chopped cilantro

Salt, to taste
1 tsp oil, to mix
2 cups oil, to fry

PREPARATION

Peel and grate raw malanga. Crush the garlic, and beat the eggs. Mix together the malanga, garlic, eggs, cilantro, salt, and 1 tsp oil.

Add 2 cups oil to a pan over heat. Carefully place a heaping spoonful of this mixture into the hot oil, and fry until golden brown.

Serve with honey for dipping.

Mojito Fruit Salad

This dish consists of mixed fruit from the island. You can really use any fruit that is in season and available at your local market.

INGREDIENTS

ORANGE, SLICED

PINEAPPLE, SLICED

STRAWBERRIES, SLICED

MANGO, SLICED

SPRIG OF MINT, CHOPPED

2 TBSP VANILLA RUM

2 TBSP BROWN SUGAR

ORANGE ZEST

PREPARATION

Mix cut fruit in a large bowl. Stir in mint. Add rum, and sprinkle with brown sugar. Garnish with orange zest, and serve.

Sofrito Salsa

Made from aromatic ingredients, such as garlic, onion, paprika, peppers, and tomatoes, this Sofrito salsa's scent wafts through many Cuban restaurants and homes. While avocado and cilantro aren't often easily found in Cuban markets, they add a nice Latin flavor to the dish.

SERVES 12
INGREDIENTS

2   TOMATOES, DICED AND SEEDED

¼   CUP DICED SMALL ONION

3   CLOVES GARLIC, PRESSED

3   CILANTRO LEAVES, MINCED

1   TBSP WHITE VINEGAR

SALT, TO TASTE

3   TBSP EXTRA-VIRGIN OLIVE OIL

½   SMALL AVOCADO, DICED

PREPARATION

Combine all of the salsa ingredients, except olive oil and avocado, in a bowl, and stir together until well combined. Cover and refrigerate for 30 minutes to let the flavors marinate.

Add extra-virgin olive oil and avocado, then stir gently so as to not mash the avocado, until well combined.

Serve with tostones (page 140).

Tostones Chatino Plantains

Tostones are a ubiquitous starter in Cuban restaurants. Known throughout Latin America as tachino, chatino, or plátano a puñetazo, this savory twice-fried plantain can be very filling and tasty. There are two types of plátanos that offer significantly different flavors—one variety looks more like a banana and is sweet, while the other is starchy and bigger. You can make chips with it, or you can boil it, mash it, and fry it to make the well-loved tostones.

INGREDIENTS

2 GREEN PLANTAINS

VEGETABLE OIL, FOR FRYING

SALT, TO TASTE

DOLLOP OF SOUR CREAM (OPTIONAL)

PREPARATION

Peel the plantains, removing the ends. Cut them in rounds that are 1–1½ inches in thickness to make the shape of a chip.

Carefully place the plantains in a pan with hot oil for approximately 7 minutes. When crisp, remove, drain, and press the plantains with a spatula to flatten until they are approximately ½ inch thick.

Raise the temperature of the oil and add the flattened plantains again. Cook for approximately 80 additional seconds.

Sprinkle with salt and serve with sofrito salsa (page 139). Add a side of sour cream if you like.

Yuca con Mojo

FRIED YUCA PATTIES

INGREDIENTS

2 LB FRESH YUCA (OR 1.5 LB FROZEN YUCA)

FILTERED WATER, FOR BOILING

1 LIME, JUICED

½ TSP UNREFINED SALT

MOJO SAUCE (SERVING: 2⅓ CUPS):

1 CUP OLIVE OIL

¾ CUP PLUS 2 TBSP FRESH LIME JUICE

¾ CUP ORANGE JUICE

½ CUP CHOPPED FRESH CILANTRO

8 GARLIC CLOVES, MINCED

1 TBSP GRATED ORANGE PEEL

1 TBSP DRIED OREGANO

2½ TSP GROUND CUMIN

1½ TSP SALT

1½ TSP GROUND BLACK PEPPER

1 SMALL WHITE OR YELLOW ONION, SLICED INTO RINGS

1 RED ONION, SLICED, TO GARNISH

Frozen yuca can actually be easier to work with then fresh, as fresh yuca skin contains hydrocyanic acid—when prepared incorrectly, it can be toxic.

PREPARATION

If using fresh yuca, peel the skin thoroughly with a knife: cut off both ends and dissect the root by cutting downward toward the board to remove the skin. Remove all traces of the pink/purple layer that is just beneath the skin as this is where the toxins are most highly concentrated. Cut peeled yuca into sections, about 3 inches long.

Add water, lime juice, and salt to a pot and bring to a boil. Add yuca pieces, then reduce heat. Let it cook uncovered for 20-30 minutes, or until easily pierced with a fork.

Prepare the mojo sauce. Whip all the ingredients for the mojo sauce in a bowl, and pour about 1 cup of the sauce into a large frying pan, along with the sliced onions. Let the onions soften over heat. Reserve the remaining sauce for another meal.

When the yuca finishes cooking, remove the tough and stringy core from each piece, and discard.

Combine the cooked, cleaned yuca and the sauce in a frying pan, and allow to simmer for 3-5 minutes, stirring on occasion. The sauce will thicken as some of the starch from the yuca cooks out.

Garnish with a sprinkling of finely sliced red onions. Serve and eat immediately as the texture will change while the yuca sits and cools.

Finca Agroecologica El Paraiso

Yuca con mojo, or yuca "with sauce," is a traditional Cuban side dish. The tastiest one I've eaten is at an organic family-run farm in Viñales called Finca Agroecologica El Paraiso. Just over a hundred miles from Havana, this farm has helped to draw tourism to the region. Wilfredo Garcia Correa and his daughters smartly grew the family business, once their private home, into a popular restaurant. With the influx of tourism over the past two years, reservations are a must, as people come from far and wide to experience the feast that the farm provides.

Only a decade ago, the land was overgrown with weeds; but now, with the help of a large crew and a brilliant foreman, the finca produces enough food to feed more than two hundred customers a day. All produce is grown on the farm, and the beef, chicken, pork, and fish are raised there or acquired through trade with local producers, depending on the season. "Organic agriculture began here in the Special Period, and it has been expanding little by little since then," Correa told me. "The Special Period provided the impetus, but we came to realize the benefits. Every year more campesinos in Viñales go organic."

There is no set menu, but if you frequent the finca often enough you'll be able to eagerly anticipate different items. The meal is brought to you plate after plate and dish after dish, and they never disappoint. Sauces are light, with the emphasis mainly on the fresh meat and vegetables. And the starchy yuca is, of course, cooked to perfection.

Organic farming in Cuba isn't a trend but rather a necessity. Farmers lack access to pesticides, leaving Cuba's rich soil among the most chemical-free in the world. Flavors come to life from the hearty soil, and the literal farm-to-table experience at the finca is one of the culinary and agriculturally educational highlights of visiting the island.

Butter Cake

Birthdays are important in Cuba, and the entire family gathers to celebrate. The most important birthday is the quinceañera, when a young woman turns fifteen. The celebration kicks off with an elaborate glamour photo shoot early in her fifteenth year, and the pictures are proudly displayed in households for many years to come. Of course, cakes are a significant aspect of any celebration in Cuba, and they are made daily for a multitude of events. A friend's aunt bakes a cake every single day and always has someone to share it with. Cakes are also offered to saints in the Santería religion.

SERVES 4
INGREDIENTS

CAKE BATTER:

1 STICK UNSALTED BUTTER, PLUS EXTRA TO GREASE RAMEKINS

4 OZ CREAM CHEESE

2¼ CUPS GRANULATED SUGAR

2 LARGE EGGS

1½ CUPS ALL-PURPOSE FLOUR

½ TSP SEA SALT

1½ TSP VANILLA EXTRACT

CREAM CHEESE LAYER:

4 OZ CREAM CHEESE

⅓ CUP GRANULATED SUGAR

1 EGG

½ TSP VANILLA EXTRACT

GUAVA JAM, TO TOP

Begin with all the ingredients at room temperature, including the eggs.

PREPARATION

Preheat the oven to 325°F. Coat 4 ramekins with butter.

Prepare the cake batter. Use an electric mixer and beat the butter, cream cheese, and sugar for 1–2 minutes. Gradually add in the eggs, one at a time, beating continuously on low until blended together.

Whisk together the flour and salt, and then add to the creamed mixture. Beat on low until mixed in, making sure not to overbeat. Add in the vanilla.

Prepare the cream cheese layer. Whip together cream cheese and granulated sugar until creamed, then add egg and vanilla extract.

Pour the cake batter into the pre-buttered ramekins, and top with a layer of the cream cheese mixture. Bake in the oven for 60–75 minutes.

Top with a thin layer of guava jam.

Chocolate Rum Ice Cream

Coppelia is Cuba's most frequented ice cream parlor and employs more than 400 residents in Havana alone. State-run, and created by Fidel Castro because of his love for dairy, it serves more than 35,000 people a day. Cubans have a sweet tooth, and ice cream is a perfect treat to combat the hot weather.

An ice cream maker and a hand mixer are needed for this recipe.

INGREDIENTS

5 oz high-quality bittersweet chocolate (70% cocoa), finely chopped	¾ cup sugar
	1½ cups whole milk
2 oz brewed espresso	1 can (12 oz) evaporated milk
6 large egg yolks	1 Tbsp dark rum

PREPARATION

Place the chocolate and freshly brewed espresso in a double boiler or a small heatproof bowl and set over a pot of simmering water. Stir until the chocolate melts, approximately 3–5 minutes. Set aside.

Using a hand mixer, rapidly beat the egg yolks and sugar until they are blended together and are form a ribbon, about 5 minutes.

Place the whole milk and evaporated milk in a medium saucepan, and bring to a simmer over medium heat. Gently add 1 cup of the heated milk to the egg yolks to temper the eggs, then add this egg mixture to the saucepan.

Whisk in the melted chocolate until it is blended with the other ingredients. Simmer over low heat, stirring constantly until it thickens and coats the back of the spoon, approximately 5 minutes.

Remove the mixture from the heat and strain into a clean mixing bowl. Stir in the rum. Cover and refrigerate for at least 3 hours.

Once chilled, remove the mixture and process in an ice cream maker for 15–20 minutes.

Cuban Pumpkin Flan

Flan is a dessert favorite and ubiquitous on menus around the island. My favorite flan is a "gas station flan" made in half-cut-off beer cans and sold at a roadside spot in Havana's neighborhood of Vedado. Much to my dismay, they stopped selling the one-dollar treat this year, but the flavor memory remains. This recipe takes the local fare to a higher level and would be a perfect use of the abundant pumpkin grown in Cuba.

SERVES: 6-8

INGREDIENTS

CUSTARD:

- 1 CUP PUMPKIN PUREE
- 1 CAN (12 OZ) EVAPORATED MILK
- 1 CAN (14 OZ) SWEETENED CONDENSED MILK
- 3 TBSP CREAM CHEESE, ROOM TEMPERATURE
- ¼ CUP GRANULATED SUGAR

- 5 EGGS
- 1 TBSP CORNSTARCH
- ½ TSP CINNAMON
- 2 TSP VANILLA EXTRACT

CARAMEL:

- 1 CUP GRANULATED SUGAR
- ¼ CUP WATER
- ½ TSP CREAM OF TARTAR

PREPARATION

Prepare your custard mixture. In a large bowl, combine the custard ingredients. Whisk until the consistency becomes smooth and custard-like, and be sure to not overbeat to avoid it becoming runny.

Strain the mixture through a fine sieve into a new, clean bowl and set aside. Preheat the oven to 300°F.

Prepare the caramel. In a medium saucepan, add sugar, water, and cream of tartar. Cook over medium heat, stirring constantly, until the sugar is dissolved, approximately 2-3 minutes. Increase the heat to medium-high and boil, without stirring, for 10 minutes, until the caramel turns to a light amber brown color.

Remove from the heat and carefully pour the caramel in a regular size flan mold. The caramel mixture will be very hot! Do this quickly. Swirl and coat the sides. Next, pour the pumpkin custard mixture over. Arrange the mold in a large deep roasting pan and pour boiling water into the roasting pan until it comes about halfway up the side of your mold.

Bake for 50-60 minutes or until a knife inserted near the center comes out clean. Remove from the oven and allow to cool for about 30 minutes. Put in the fridge for several hours before serving.

Dulce de Leche

Dulce de leche is a Cuban favorite, and one of my favorites, too. The sweet flavor comes from the process of slowly heating the milk. The dessert's name literally means "candy of milk."

SERVES 8

INGREDIENTS

1 CAN (14 OZ) SWEETENED CONDENSED MILK, UNOPENED

PREPARATION

Peel the label off the can of sweetened condensed milk, and place it in a pot. Cover it with water about 1-2 inches over the top of the can. Bring to a gentle boil, then reduce the heat to low, letting the water come to a slow simmer. If the level of water falls below the top of the can, add more water to the pot.

For a lighter dulce, simmer the can for 2-2½ hours; for a darker and more flavorful dulce, simmer for 3½ hours. *Very carefully* turn over the cans halfway through the simmering process.

Turn off the heat and allow the cans to come to room temperature. Cool them completely before opening. Stir the dulce de leche, and serve.

Natilla Custard

Similar to the Spanish crema Catalana, natilla custard is a fantastic traditional Cuban substitute for your dessert flan.

INGREDIENTS

4 CUPS WHOLE MILK

2-INCH STRIP LEMON, ZESTED

1 CINNAMON STICK

¼ TSP SALT

1¼ CUPS GRANULATED SUGAR

8 LARGE EGG YOLKS

¼ CUP CORNSTARCH, DISSOLVED IN ¼ CUP WATER

1 TSP PURE VANILLA EXTRACT

GROUND CINNAMON, FOR GARNISH

POWDERED SUGAR, FOR GARNISH (OPTIONAL)

PREPARATION

In a large saucepan, combine the milk with the lemon zest, cinnamon stick, and salt. Bring to a simmer.

In a large bowl, beat the granulated sugar with the egg yolks at medium speed until they are pale, approximately 4 minutes. Beat in the cornstarch mixture until blended. Turn the mixer to a low speed, and gradually beat in half of the hot milk mixture.

Pour the egg-and-milk mixture into the saucepan and cook the custard over moderate heat, whisking constantly for 18 minutes, until it is very thick. Whisk in the vanilla. Transfer the custard to a large bowl, and discard the cinnamon stick.

Cover the surface of the custard with plastic wrap (it is okay if it touches the custard) and refrigerate until chilled, approximately 3 hours. Spoon the custard into 6 bowls, and top with a dusting of ground cinnamon. Add powdered sugar to the top, if you like.

The egg custard can be refrigerated for up to 3 days, which makes it an easy dessert to pre-prep for a party.

Shredded Coconut

Dessert doesn't have to always be rich and caloric to be flavorful. With an abundance of coconut and papaya on the island, this is an easy, affordable treat.

INGREDIENTS

1   FRESH COCONUT

CINNAMON, TO TASTE

1   FRESH PAPAYA, SLICED OR CUBED

2   TBSP SUGAR

PREPARATION

Chop open the coconut with a large knife. Pout out the milk and set aside. Shred the coconut flesh into a bowl. Top with cinnamon to taste and papaya, and drizzle with the coconut milk. Add a dash of sugar for additional sweetness.

Plátanos En Tentación

CARAMEL-GLAZED PLANTAINS

My favorite side dish or Cuban dessert, caramelized plantains can be paired with sweet or savory meals. If you serve it as a side with meat and rice, the sweetness of the caramelization brings a roundness of flavors to the experience. If you serve it as a dessert, try adding a generous scoop of vanilla ice cream on the side. Either way, the gooey, warm sweetness of the dish is a household and restaurant favorite across the island.

INGREDIENTS

3 RIPE BANANAS OR PLANTAINS	6 Tbsp BROWN SUGAR
¼ STICK OF BUTTER	2 CINNAMON STICKS
WATER, FOR THE PAN	GROUND CINNAMON, TO GARNISH

PREPARATION

Cut each banana into 4 pieces. Sauté in the butter, turning constantly. Let them brown on all sides.

Add water to cover the banana, filling the pan halfway up the sides. Add the brown sugar and the pieces of cinnamon, and let it boil.

Wait until the mixture thickens, like a caramel. The bananas should be completely cooked. Sprinkle the top with ground cinnamon.

Torticas De Moron

GUAVA SUGAR COOKIES

Sweets are common in Cuba. They are consumed any time of the day, and not just as a post-meal treat. Locals sell their baked goods from street windows, in hand-carried boxes while they walk down the avenues, or in the backs of small carts. Most are delicious, and freshly baked cookies with guava are a particularly tasty dessert.

SERVINGS: 4 DOZEN
INGREDIENTS

- 3 CUPS FLOUR, PLUS EXTRA
- 1½ TSP BAKING POWDER
- 1 TSP GROUND CINNAMON
- ½ TSP KOSHER SALT
- ⅔ CUP PACKED LIGHT BROWN SUGAR
- 16 TBSP UNSALTED BUTTER, SOFTENED
- 1 EGG

- 1 TBSP FRESH LIME JUICE
- 2 TBSP WHITE RUM
- 6 OZ GUAVA PASTE OR JAM, WARMED UNTIL SOFT
- 2 OZ CREAM CHEESE, SOFTENED
- SEA SALT OR FLEUR DE SEL, TO SPRINKLE

PREPARATION

Stir together the flour, baking powder, cinnamon, and salt in a bowl, and set aside.

In another bowl, beat the sugar and butter on medium-high speed using a hand mixer until fluffy. Add the egg, and mix until smooth. Add in the flour mixture, lime juice, and rum, and mix until combined.

Transfer to a dry, floured work surface and shape the dough into a disk. Wrap with plastic wrap and refrigerate until firm, at least 2 hours or overnight.

Heat the oven to 350°F. Transfer the ready-made dough to a dry, floured work surface and roll out until it is approximately ¼ inch thick. Using a 2-inch-wide scalloped cutter, cut out the cookies, and place them 2 inches apart on a parchment paper–lined baking sheets.

Bake in the oven until the edges are lightly golden, approximately 15 minutes. Let cool completely.

Whisk the guava paste and cream cheese together in a bowl until smooth. Transfer to a plastic bag and snip off a small corner piece of the bag. Pipe about 1 tsp of the mixture on top of each cookie. Sprinkle with sea salt or fleur de sel before serving.

Panqueque de Maíz con Mango

CORN PANCAKES WITH MANGO BUTTER

I love fruit spreads for pancakes, and mango is the perfect flavor for summer. Cuba's markets and street vendors have an abundance of the sweet fruit, and it is very common in Havana to serve mango or papaya with breakfast and dessert.

SERVES 4
INGREDIENTS

MANGO BUTTER:

1 WHOLE RIPE MANGO, PEELED

1 CUP UNSALTED BUTTER, ROOM TEMPERATURE

HONEY, TO DRIZZLE

PANCAKE MIX:

1 CUP YELLOW CORN

3 LARGE EGGS

1½ CUPS BUTTERMILK

5 TBSP BUTTER, MELTED

1¼ CUPS FINELY GROUND YELLOW CORNMEAL

1¼ CUPS ALL-PURPOSE FLOUR

⅓ CUP BROWN SUGAR

1 TBSP BAKING POWDER

1 TSP BAKING SODA

¾ TSP SALT

3 TBSP VEGETABLE OIL, FOR THE GRIDDLE

PREPARATION

Prepare the mango butter. Finely chop or puree the flesh of a whole ripe mango in a blender or food processor.

Mix ½ cup of the pureed mango with the butter. Add a drizzle of honey and stir in. Refrigerate until ready for use.

Prepare the pancake mix. Pulse the corn in a food processor until ground into a smooth paste. Beat the eggs in a large bowl until they have a consistently blended texture. Add the ground corn, buttermilk, and butter, and blend until smooth.

In a separate bowl, blend the cornmeal, flour, brown sugar, baking powder, baking soda, and salt. Once combined, add this into the egg mixture until you have a batter. If necessary, add an additional splash of buttermilk.

Preheat a skillet on the stove with oil over low to medium heat. Take heaping spoonfuls of the pancake mixture and place into the pan. Flip once so both sides are golden brown.

Serve immediately with the mango butter.

Bebidas

*My mojito in the Bodeguita del Medio,
my daiquiri in the Floridita.*
—ERNEST HEMINGWAY

While Hemingway's favorites are certainly classic cocktail bars, and we have them to thank for the creation of the daiquiri and the mojito, Cuba's cocktail club culture has progressed in the past few years to more interesting creations and is on par with some of the best spots throughout the world. El Cocinero, a lively rooftop restaurant that is adjacent to the famed art and music space Fábrica de Arte Cubano (FAC), is the perfect spot to sip on something cool on a hot day. The heaping icy creations from La Lamparilla are a favorite, and star mixologist Wilson Hernandez serves up Cuba's tastiest libations at El Del Frente and 304 O'Reilly. The rooftop bars at Roma and La Guarida are not to be missed either, and both draw crowds of locals and tourists alike. Havana's cocktail scene is lively and hip.

My first "mixology" experience in Cuba was on a quiet day in early October 2012, before tourists freely flooded the streets of Havana. Obama was in office, and even though I had visited before, the cocktails I had had before seemed to be a sugary mix of lime and Coke, at best. The heat in October can be oppressive, and my thirst and hunger took a turn for the worse.

Wilson M. Hernandez, with his wild hair and friendly face, stood behind the small bar at 304 O'Reilly, an unassuming space with fewer than six tables. When I saw his drinks—large, overflowing glasses of pinks and yellows; frozen ice and condensation dripping slowly down the sides; topped with fresh watermelon slices, pineapple, cherries, and lime—I knew that I had finally found my "Havana local" to call home.

What I saw in the bar has been recognized by many others since, and its popularity has necessitated a second space across the street. El Del Frente is run primarily by Wilson, and its kitchen staff work tirelessly to fulfill the demand of its stream of patrons.

"Jose Carlos Imperatori is the main brain," Wilson modestly reminded me from time to time, referring to El Del Frente's owner. But I laughed and told him that he has become the "face" of the Cuban cocktail scene. He jokingly corrected me and said he is actually its "soul." Even Airbnb, a hospitality service that allows users to lease or rent out their living spaces, prominently features Wilson's face and biography as their "cocktail impresario" of sorts for Cuba.

Jose Carlos was a student under Cuba's top chef, Thomas Erasmo Hernandez Leon, who worked at La Ferminia and El Tocororo. There, he learned the essential skills to run a successful kitchen and restaurant, and then branched out on his own, creating O'Riley 304 O'Reilly.

Wilson studied Jose Carlos's ways, and improved himself behind the bar. He learned music and art from Jose Carlos, who taught Wilson how to find customers, and even locations. "He is my mentor," said Wilson of Jose Carlos, "my everything."

The two have grown in their tastes and skills together as well, and when they started El Del Frente, it was an instant success. Their friendships with owners and chefs at Cuba's best restaurants have also greatly influenced them.

To make anything work in Cuba, you have to be a maverick and a MacGyver. "Everything in the restaurant is from Cuba, but repurposed," Wilson said to me, as different men came to our table showing him fresh fish or antiques that he might like for the restaurant. This happens daily, and Wilson is decisive in his taste. "Yes to the fish, and yes to the light fixture. No to the chair and clock." He continued, "Different purveyors make essential items. One guy makes coconut milk for us. Ours is the best that you will find on the island as it has coconut milk, powdered milk, and sugar (of course, we cannot give you the secret recipe). Another guy makes our celery salt. Four or five guys provide the antiques for the restaurant—the jars that the potatoes came in. I decided to use them as drink glasses because we couldn't get any good matching glasses anywhere."

The cocktails certainly draw a crowd, and Wilson's enigmatic personality and quirkiness keep people coming back time and time again. Young, hip Cubans with disposable money from tourism jobs mingle with travelers, and El Del Frente continues to innovate recipes and grow.

When asked about the future of food in Cuba, Wilson seems excited and hopeful. His travels have taken him to Europe, Miami, and New York, and the developing cult following for 304 and Frente will help. On the table is a need to improve the kitchen and to continue to study the craft of the cocktail.

Cuba has always been known for cocktails, but Wilson clarified. "We were the first to make this kind of cocktails, using the mason jars. We opened a bridge to what's happening in cocktail culture around the world, especially in the US." Wilson and Jose Carlos have a sizable library of cocktail books, and they have taken influence from others in Cuba's top restaurants. Wilson's grandmother, who is almost a hundred years old, continues to inspire and guide him.

Like all others, Wilson and El Del Frente's evolution comes partly from need. "You can't find coffee glasses anywhere in Cuba right now," he says, as we sip from small jars. "I like these," I say. "Thanks. Large baby food glass jars—for coffee. Ha!" We smile and laugh, and I know I am welcome here anytime.

Café Cubano

(NON-ALCOHOLIC DRINK)

Cuban coffee is such a staple of Cuban society that is difficult to imagine finishing off a large meal without it. Often café Cubano is enjoyed with a hand-rolled cigar, a chair in the shade, and the sound of Cuban rhythms in the air. A favorite spot for this is the Café Paris in Havana's Old Town; a place where locals and visitors mix as they come for the live music and the opportunity to watch passersby walk from square to square. I love to go there in the early evenings when the temperature drops just a bit. At this time, the corner café usually picks up a slight breeze, and makes enjoying the music and the hustle and bustle of the crowd enough entertainment for the night.

INGREDIENTS

GROUND ESPRESSO
¼ CUP SUGAR
MOKA POT

PREPARATION

Brew a pot of espresso on the stove top in a Moka pot. Measure out the sugar in a large glass measuring cup, and add 1 Tbsp of the hot espresso.

Using a small whisk, beat the sugar with the espresso until they combine and turn pale and thick and the sugar is nearly dissolved, approximately 1 minute. Stir in the remaining hot espresso. Let the foam rise to the top, then pour into espresso cups and serve immediately.

Avispa

Avispa is also known as the "yellow jacket" cocktail because of its powerful sting. It was made famous at El Floridita.

INGREDIENTS

3 OZ HOT MILK

1 TSP WHITE SUGAR

1½ OZ WHITE RUM

2 CLOVES

1 STAR ANISE, TO GARNISH

PREPARATION

Heat the milk and pour it into a thick old-fashioned glass. Add sugar, rum, and cloves. Gently stir all the ingredients together. Garnish with the star anise and serve.

Canchanchara

Created for Cubans to "withstand the difficulty" of the war for independence against Spain, this cocktail is considered to be the "grandfather" of the mojito and the daiquiri.

INGREDIENTS

2 TSP HONEY
½ OZ LEMON JUICE
2 OZ CANE LIQUOR

ICE CUBES
LIME WEDGE, TO GARNISH IF DESIRED

PREPARATION

Mix the honey and the lemon juice in a cup. Add the cane liquor. Pour over ice and stir. Garnish with a lime wedge.

Caipirinha Havana, El Del Frente

Wilson's take on the Brazilian Caipirinha, this strong drink is bitter and sweet.

INGREDIENTS

½ LIME
1 TSP WHITE SUGAR
2.5 OZ CACHAÇA

1 CUP ICE CUBES
1 PINEAPPLE WEDGE

PREPARATION

Squeeze lime into a large glass. Add sugar, and crush and mix with a spoon. Pour in the cachaça and plenty of ice. Stir well. Garnish with a pineapple wedge.

Classic Daiquiri, El Floridita

Created in the streets of Havana at Floridita, the daiquiri has been a favorite of visitors and locals for decades.

INGREDIENTS

¼ CUP LIGHT RUM (HAVANA CLUB, IF YOU CAN GET THE REAL THING)

1 FL OZ LIME JUICE

4 TBSP OF SIMPLE SYRUP

ICE CUBES

PINEAPPLE SLICE, TO GARNISH

PREPARATION

Pour all ingredients except the pineapple into a shaker and shake until cold. For this drink, the balance between sweet and sour is key. Strain into a pre-chilled glass, and garnish with a slice of fresh pineapple.

Crema de Vie

CUBAN EGGNOG

Holidays are an important aspect of Cuba's family-focused culture, and the eggnog recipe is commonly made during Christmas when families gather.

INGREDIENTS

2 CUPS SUGAR

1 CUP WATER

2 PEELS LEMON RIND (FROM ¼ LEMON)

1 CINNAMON STICK

½ VANILLA BEAN, SPLIT

6 EGG YOLKS

1 CAN (14 OZ) SWEETENED CONDENSED MILK

1 TSP VANILLA

½ CUP RUM (OR COGNAC)

1 MARASCHINO CHERRY, TO GARNISH

PREPARATION

Make a simple syrup by placing sugar, water, lemon rind, cinnamon stick, and vanilla bean in a pot. Bring to a simmer over medium-high heat for about a minute, stirring constantly to avoid boiling over. Remove from heat and let cool completely.

Strain the contents into a large bowl or pitcher. Whisk egg yolks and strain into a separate bowl. Add the strained egg yolks, condensed milk, vanilla, and rum to the simple syrup and whisk thoroughly.

Pass the final mixture through a clean strainer two more times, then refrigerate until cold. Serve with a maraschino cherry, and enjoy.

Cuba Bella

Another creation from the famed El Floridita, this cocktail's sweet grenadine quality is a nod to the 1950s cocktail party scene.

INGREDIENTS

4 OR 5 ICE CUBES

½ OZ GRENADINE SYRUP

1 OZ MINT LIQUEUR

½ OZ LEMON JUICE

2 OZ SODA WATER

2 OZ RUM BLONDE

MINT, TO GARNISH

1 CHERRY OR MORELLO CHERRY, TO GARNISH

PREPARATION

Put the ice into a glass. Add the other ingredients, one at a time, and allow them to remain layered and unmixed. Add mint to the top. Garnish with a cherry place on the rim of the glass.

Cuba Libre

"FREE CUBA"

The Cuba Libre, rum and Coke with lime, is the national drink of Cuba. Though it has conflicting stories of origin, this drink is generally believed to date back to the 1900s when Coca-Cola first entered the Cuban market.

INGREDIENTS

ICE CUBES

10 TSP LIGHT RUM

2 TSP FRESHLY SQUEEZED LIME JUICE

4 FL OZ COCA-COLA

1 LIME, TO GARNISH

PREPARATION

Fill glass with ice and pour over rum, lime juice, and Coca-Cola. Garnish with a slice of lime.

Cubanacan

The name means "where fertile land is abundant," and it comes from tobacco traditions.

INGREDIENTS

3 OZ ANGOSTURA BITTERS

½ OZ RED VERMOUTH

1½ OZ AGED WHITE RUM

LEMON PEEL, TO GARNISH

PREPARATION

Pour the ingredients into a shaker and mix for approximately 10 seconds until chilled. Serve in a low cocktail glass, and garnish with a lemon peel.

Havana Especial

A mix of sweet and citrus flavors.

INGREDIENTS

½ OZ AGED WHITE RUM

1½ OZ PINEAPPLE JUICE

1 TSP MARASCHINO LIQUEUR

ICE

1 PINEAPPLE SLICE

PREPARATION

Mix all of the ingredients except the pineapple in a shaker. Strain and serve in a cocktail glass. Garnish with a pineapple slice.

Havana London from El Del Frente

Wilson's London visit inspired this unique drink. A different take on the traditional daiquiri.

INGREDIENTS

Daiquiri (page 177)

1.5 oz Curacao (use a jigger to measure)

1 Tbsp gin

5½ Tbsp tonic water

2 red cherries

PREPARATION

In a blender, make daiquiris (page 177) and add in the curacao, gin, and tonic water. Blend together until the mix is blue. Top with cherries. The cocktail will be red, white, blue.

Pesca's, El Del Frente

Sangria is the best way to use excess fruit. Let the wine soak into the berries, oranges, etc., and enjoy this drink on a hot day.

INGREDIENTS

Ice, to fill a pitcher

½ bottle white table wine

1 tsp simple syrup

1 Tbsp lemon juice

4 Tbsp sparkling water

Assortment of sliced fruits, e.g. orange, lemon, grape, berry (as much as you like to fill the pitcher)

½ bottle red table wine

PREPARATION

Fill a pitcher with ice and add white wine on the bottom. Mix in simple syrup, lemon juice, and sparkling water. Add in the sliced fruit. Fill the top half of the pitcher with red wine. Gently stir with a wooden spoon and serve.

Piña Colada

A classic Caribbean drink, the best piña coladas on the island are made by the bar staff at La Lamparilla, where the view from the rooftop bar sweeps over the Havana streets and ends at the horizon over the bay.

INGREDIENTS

1   OZ COCONUT CREAM
2   OZ PINEAPPLE JUICE
1½ CUP AGED WHITE RUM
BLENDED ICE (FRAPPE)

1   PINEAPPLE SLICE, TO GARNISH

PREPARATION

Put the ingredients except the pineapple in a blender and blend on high. Once ready, pour into a glass and garnish with a pineapple slice.

Piña Colada, O'Reilly

A TWIST ON THE CLASSIC FAVORITE

INGREDIENTS

¼   CUP GRENADINE AND SUGAR MIX, TO COAT RIM
4   OR 5 ICE CUBES

1   PINA COLADA MIX (ABOVE)
1   PINEAPPLE SLICE, TO GARNISH

PREPARATION

Dip the rim of the glass into the mix of grenadine and sugar. Add the ice, then fill the glass with the pina colada mixture. Garnish with slice of pineapple.

Café Fortuna Joe

My first visit to Café Fortuna Joe was a surprising one. Tucked within the second floor of a modest building in Miramar, overlooking the northern part of the Caribbean Sea, one would never think that such a treasure was hidden inside. Like so many restaurants in Cuba, you have to be in the know to find them, and making friends with locals is the only way to truly stay in the know.

My young friend, Alejandro, who knows me well, gleefully said, "I have somewhere to take you that you have never been." I chuckled, mistakenly dubious after so much time spent on the island, but I was ready to see something new.

Outside, a balcony stretches along the building wall with a thick blue-and-white striped canopy that protects patrons from the blazing sun, painting a picture of something decidedly French. Inside, typewriters and chandeliers make up the eclectic interior of antiques from the 1800s and 1950s. The seats range from wood furnishings to a vintage horse carriage and half of a 1950s Chevy car. Waiters in grey-and-white striped shirts with white pants and blue aprons flank the breezy deck with its graffiti-covered ceiling and tile floor. Food and cocktails for the young crowd are priced well, and locals enjoy the scene.

I love Fortuna Joe. It was my missing Cuban puzzle piece—a bar near the water where you can listen to the lapping of waves as you drink with young locals to catch up on the daily news. It is in many ways a perfect spot.

Pineapple Mojito

A sweet island twist to the classic Cuban cocktail.

INGREDIENTS

SIMPLE SYRUP:

1 CUP WATER

2 CUPS SUGAR

COCKTAIL:

12 MINT LEAVES

2 OZ FRESH PINEAPPLE CHUNKS

ICE CUBES

2 OZ PINEAPPLE-COCONUT RUM

1 OZ FRESH LIME JUICE

½ OZ ORANGE LIQUEUR

1 PINEAPPLE SLICE, TO GARNISH

PREPARATION

Prepare the simple syrup. Heat water and sugar in a small saucepan until the sugar is dissolved. Bring to a boil, and then set aside to cool.

Prepare the cocktail. In a Collins glass, muddle the mint leaves and pineapple chunks. Fill with ice. In a cocktail shaker, shake together rum, lime juice, 1 oz of the simple syrup, and orange liqueur. Strain into the glass and garnish with a slice of fresh pineapple.

Rum Frappé

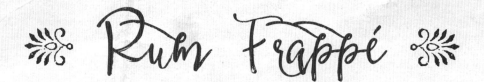

The perfect iced drink.

INGREDIENTS

1½ OZ AGED RUM

¼ OZ LEMON JUICE

½ OZ CRÈME DE CACAO

BLENDED ICE (FRAPPE)

LEMON ZEST, TO GARNISH

PREPARATION

Pour all of the ingredients except lemon zest into a blender and blend. Pour out and serve in a champagne coupe. Garnish with lemon zest.

Saoco

The mixture of coconuts and alcohol was used as a tonic by Cuban slaves when they were working the sugarcane fields. It is now a popular drink in Havana.

INGREDIENTS

1   COCONUT (TO USE AS A VESSEL)

4   OZ COCONUT WATER

2   OZ AGED WHITE RUM OR CANE LIQUOR

ICE

CHERRY, TO GARNISH

PREPARATION

Cut a coconut in half and drain the juice. Put the ingredients except the cherry in one half of the coconut, using it as a container. Stir the mixture, garnish with a cherry, and serve it with a straw.

Torres Especial

A creamy cocktail that dates back to the 1950s. The mint cream and cocoa cream make this a dessert-like drink.

INGREDIENTS

½   OZ MINT CREAM

½   OZ CRÈME DE CACAO

½   OZ WHITE VERMOUTH

½   OZ SPECIAL AGED RUM

ICE

ANGOSTURA BITTERS, TO SPRINKLE

PREPARATION

Put the mint cream in the base of a flute glass. Pour the remaining ingredients except for the ice and angostura into a cocktail shaker, and shake for 30 seconds. Next, fill the flute glass with ice and pour the contents of the shaker over the ice. Sprinkle the drink with a dash of angostura.

Cigars

Cuban cigars, according to many experts, are the finest in the world. They have always been a coveted and valued commodity on the island. Anyone with a real Cuban cigar can illegally sell or trade them in most countries for real profit.

The tobacco grown in Cuba benefits from the extremely humid climate and chemical-free fertile soil. Cuban national hero José Martí was known to say that tobacco plants had to be "handled as carefully as if they were fine ladies."

The process is not easy. The cultivation of tobacco begins in the seedbed, where seedlings germinate for forty days until they are transplanted to the fields. The seedlings are then planted in stages, beginning in October. The leaves are picked between forty-five and eighty days later. Next, the tobacco leaves are taken into the curing barns, where they are hung to ferment and dry. Workers in the sorting houses are selected for their skill, and it is a coveted job. Many are women, who delicately select and sort the leaves without breaking them.

Leaves are sorted into those that will be used as wrappers and those that will become the filling. Each leaf is sorted by size and color, and this is done one at a time through a process of hand smoothing, pulling, and rubbing to ensure that everything is perfect. The leaves that are later used as wrappers are gently sprinkled with water to restore some humidity and strengthen them for the rolling process.

Next, the cigar maker takes the leaves, places them on the table, selects different leaves for each function (wrapping, filling), and shapes them into a bundle. The bundle is smoothed, trimmed, and wrapped, all by hand.

The flat side of a sharp knife is pressed along the rolled cigar, and the end of the cigar is shaped. Then, the nearly finished cigar is placed in a cutter, and the tip is clipped for length.

Once the habanos (Cuban-made cigars) are approved for sale, they are tied into groups of fifty and put into a vacuum chamber to properly fumigate. Next, the cigars are placed in a special closet for three weeks to remove excess humidity. After this the cigars are taken to yet another inspection level. When the final cigars are chosen, a cigar band is placed around each one and they are taken to be sold.

RESTAURANTS

Atelier

Calle 5 | between Paseo and Calle 2 | Vedado

+53 7 8362025

Some of the finest cuisine on the island, Atelier could rival any Michelin-starred restaurant in the US. A former mansion turned fine dining venue, Atelier is well worth a visit.

Café Paris

San Ignacio and Obispo streets | Old Havana

+53 7 8620466

When you are strolling through the streets of Havana, the beating drums of music cannot help but lure you in. Here, you can sit outside and listen to music for hours.

Casa Miglis

Lealtad 120 | between Animas and Lagunas | Havana Centro

+53 7 8641486

Havana's version of the House of Blues, Miglis is by far my favorite way to begin any visit. With fantastic food and live music, this intimate restaurant, situated in an old mansion, is a perfect way to be welcomed into Cuba.

Doña Eutimia

Callejón del Chorro No 60c | Plaza de la Catedral | Old Havana

+53 7 8611332

A renowned Cuban restaurant, Eutimia is positioned off the most charming of Havana's four squares (Cathedral). Surrounded by art galleries and competing eateries, Doña Eutimia captures the best flavors of the traditional Cuban dish.

Elite

705 38 St. | between 42 and 7ma | Miramar
+53 7 2093260

Perhaps the most formal fine dining experience on the island, Elite is a 1980s throwback worth a visit. The black and white décor, the staff clad in tuxedos, and the meticulously plated dishes are simply something you no longer see in the US. The food is top-notch, and the neighborhood is well off the tourist path.

El Cocinero

Calle 26 | between 11 and 13 | Vedado
+53 7 8322355

Another fantastic rooftop bar and restaurant, El Cocinero is well worth a visit. Relax here on a hot day and enjoy the breeze as you look over the buildings. It is located in the same building as FAC.

El Del Frente

O'Reilly 303 | Havana
+53 7 8630206

With trendy food, a rooftop bar, and the best cocktails on the island, this is what modern Cuba is all about. It is located across the street from its sister bar, 304 O'Reilly.

Finca Agroecologica El Paraiso | Viñales

Carretera Al Cementerio KM 1 ½
+53 5 8188581

By far my favorite spot on the island, this farm-to-table experience is worth the drive (2½ hours from Havana).

Habana 61

Calle Habana No. 61 | between Cuarteles and Peña Pobre | Havana
+53 7 8016433

A Cuban classic meal with an intimate atmosphere, this spot is perfect for a romantic dinner.

La Guarida

Concordia #418 | Havana Centro

+53 7 8669047

The most famous restaurant in Cuba. Premier place for a sunset on the rooftop bar! Swanky lounge atmosphere where young Cubans and tourists mix. It was featured in the movie *Fresa y Chocolate*.

Mediterraneo

406 13th St | between F and G | Vedado

+53 7 8324894

Some of the best food you will find. Mediterraneo's old mansion interior and formal staff just add to the experience.

Paladar Vistamar

Avenida 1ra No. 2206 | between 22 and 24 | Miramar

+53 7 2038328

With a view like this you simply cannot go wrong. One of Cuba's few restaurants by the water, Vistamar never disappoints, and the staff is lovely, too.

Río Mar

3ra and Final # 11, La Puntilla | Miramar

+53 7 2094838

More fine dining than hip eats, but the views are beautiful as the restaurant sits on the water. This spot is inside a mid-century modern house.

Restaurante Paladar Decameron

Linea Number 753 | Vedado

+53 7 8322444

Off the tourist path in the charming neighborhood of Vedado, Decameron's feel is 1950s Italian. The pastas are made to perfection, and the seafood is their specialty.

BARS

304 O'Reilly

O'Reilly #304 | Havana

+53 5 2644725

With the best cocktails on the island by far, 304 O'Reilly is situated across the street from its sister restaurant, El Del Frente. The food here is delectibly fresh and some of the best you will find in Cuba.

Restaurant 1830

Calzada and Calle 20 | Vedado

+53 7 553090

Bar Roma

Aguacate 162 | O'Reilly and San Juan de Dios | Havana

Ask around and you will find this unmarked rooftop bar, which was once the balcony of a private apartment. The bathroom is still inside of a dilapidated working apartment, where and you can see how many Havanans still live.

El Bohemio

Calle 21 | Havana

+53 7 8336918

El Floridita

Obispo No.557 | Calle Obispo | Havana

+53 7 8671300

This is the famous Hemingway bar that put Havana's cocktail culture on the map. It is one drink only, which is enough as the drinks are sweet and the bar is a constant bustle of tourists. That said, it wouldn't be a visit to Havana without stepping in and having a drink; a must-see!

Espacios

Calle 10 | Vedado

+53 7 2022921

An outdoor bar with wood-fired pizza. This is a favorite for many locals in Vedado.

Fábrica de Arte Cubano (FAC)
Calle 26 | Havana
+53 7 8382260

Cuba's bustling art and music scene collide in this nightclub-cum-art-gallery. The sandwiches here are the best in the country, so be sure to have one when you take a rest from the crowd.

La Bodeguita del Medio
Empedrado No. 207 | between Cuba and San Ignacio | Havana
+53 7 8671374

Come for a drink in this renowned Havana spot and mingle with the overflowing crowd that lines the narrow street. Bring a pen and sign your name on the wall next to legends like Hemingway and others.

La Guarida Rooftop Bar
418 Concordia | Havana
+53 7 8669047

Havana's most famed restaurant now has a rooftop bar that rivals any view in the city. Come for sunset and stay for one of the best meals in town.

Lamparilla Tapas & Cervezas
Lamparilla 361 | between Aguacate and Villegas | Havana
+53 5 2895324

A kitschy, eclectic spot full of vintage pieces like telephones and typewriters, complete with a modern décor. The bar sits inside a former garage with doors that pull up. The drinks are enormous, with heaping ice and fresh fruit. One of my favorite spots.

Submarine Amarillo (Yellow Submarine)
Calle 17 and 6 | Havana
+53 7 8306808

The best music cover bands you will ever hear in your life perform here nightly; the Rolling Stones and the Beatles would be proud. All musicians in Cuba are classically trained, and the bands at the Yellow Submarine are among the most talented of the bunch. Note: Western rock music was banned in Cuba until only a decade ago.

LOCALS' FAVORITES (AND MINE, TOO)

Las Duenas

Wieros

Street pizza

Cafeterias in Old Havana

Liza's favorite eight-day-seven-night itinerary at a glance

Day 1: Arrive in Havana
- Money exchange
- Check in to accommodations
- Refresh
- Dinner / Cocktails at Casa Miglis
- Hotel, Havana

Day 2: Old Havana
- Breakfast
- Old Havana city tour (easy to find local guides for the day)
- Artist studio tour at the Experimental Graphic Art Studio on Cathedral Square
- Lunch at Doña Eutimia next to Graphic Art Studio
- Artist museums in Old Havana
- Afternoon cocktail / coffee on the roof of a hotel, or on the streets of Havana
- Hotel to freshen up for night on the town
- Late dinner / experience / dancing: Fabrica de Arte Cubano (Thursday–Sunday nights)
- Hotel, Havana

Day 3: Viñales
- Breakfast in hotel
- Depart for overnight trip (Cubarizon offers trips for US$250)
- Arrive at Las Terrazas (1½ hours driving time) for view and boating or canopy tour
- Arrival at Viñales (2½ hours total from Havana)
- Lunch at organic farm Finca Agroecologica
- Viñales town
- Refresh
- Dinner in the town square
- Outdoor salsa club with live performance on the square
- Hotel, Viñales

Day 4: Viñales / Havana
- Breakfast at casa
- Horseback ride through countryside of Viñales
- Lunch at a local stop, on horse back ride
- Car trip back to Havana
- Dinner at Starbien
- Dance Club 1830 / Havana Bar Roma
- Hotel, Havana

Day 5: Trinidad
- Drive to Trinidad (4½ hours total)
- Picnic lunch at scenic spot
- Bay of Pigs swim / beach time

- Check in to hotel in Trinidad
- Explore town
- Dinner in town
- Dancing at Trinidad's famous Cave Bar
- Hotel, Trinidad

Day 6: Trinidad

- Breakfast in town
- Explore local markets/galleries
- Horse carts to the waterfall
- Picnic lunch at the waterfall
- Return to hotel to freshen up
- Dinner in town at local choice
- Live music on the main square
- Hotel, Trinidad

Day 7: Drive to Havana/ final night

- Breakfast in hotel
- Drive towards Havana
- Stop at Cienfuegos Yacht Club for harbor view and lunch
- Optional swim
- Continue drive to Havana
- Refresh
- Cocktail sunset at La Guardia (make a reservation in advance!)
- Final dinner at La Guarida
- Hotel, Havana

Day 8: Depart

- Depart Havana for home

BEFORE YOU GO

CHECK YOUR TRAVEL DOCUMENTS

- *Are they up to date? Some countries do not allow you to travel if your passport is expiring within 6 months of departure.*
- *Do you need a flight?*
- *Do you have a valid passport?*
- *Do you have travel insurance?*

General Information

TO PACK

Documents:

- Passport (with three photocopies)
- Travel insurance (with three photocopies)
- Airline tickets (with three photocopies)
- Other IDs

Clothing:

- Swim cover-up
- Swimwear
- Light rain jacket
- Walking shoes
- Flip-flops
- 4 nighttime outfits (a bit nicer than day outfits—dresses, collared shirts)
- 1 pair long pants that can be worn to a nicer dinner (men)
- Closed-toe non-running shoes (don't bring heels as the streets are cobblestone)
- Shirts, shorts, dresses, etc.
- Light sweater / jacket for air conditioning

Toiletries:

- Sunscreen
- Medication
- Anti-diarrhea / laxative
- Pepto-Bismol
- Antibiotics
- Feminine hygiene products
- Razors
- Deodorant
- Toothpaste and toothbrush
- Shampoo and conditioner
- Bug spray

Miscellaneous:

- Beach towel
- Sunglasses (I like to bring two pairs)
- Hat
- Hot sauce, if that's your thing (hot sauces are hard to find in Cuba)
- Book to read at the beach / during downtime (you won't be able to use your smartphone for Wi-Fi or text entertainment, so download anything beforehand)
- Umbrella
- Toilet paper / wipes

Devices if you can't break away:

- Phone and charger, works with US plugs
- Camera, charger, and memory sticks

MONEY & CURRENCY

There are two official currencies in Cuba. The convertible peso (CUC) and the Cuban peso (CUP or moneda nacional [MN]). The exchange rates of these currencies are fixed by the Cuban government; however, they are liable to change at any time.

As a tourist, nearly all of your transactions we will be using the CUC. Presently, the CUC is at a fixed rate of CUC$1 = US$1. With exchange, it is approximately CUC$1 = US$1.13.

Remember:

Your credit card will not work.

Your ATM card will not work.

You cannot get cash from a bank.

The cash you bring is the cash you have.

Tips:

There will be times during you trip when there are opportunities to tip local guides, musicians, waiters, taxi drivers, etc. This is a completely optional practice to show your appreciation for excellent service.

SHOPPING

Remember to get a receipt before purchasing any valuable souvenirs in Cuba as this allows you to export them duty-free.

Cigars

Cohibas cigars are said to be the best, and hence they are the most expensive. Other notable brands are Corona, Montecristo, Partagas, Hoyo de Monterrey, H. Upmann, and Romeo y Julieta.

Guayaberas

Guayaberas, men's pleated tropical shirt, have become more or less the national dress. They can be purchased almost everywhere.

Rum

Rum is arguably the best in the world and costs from $2 to $85 per bottle.

ART

FUSTERLANDIA Cuban artist José Fuster has created an entire neighborhood from tile shapes and bright colors. His work has been compared to Picasso, and the neighborhood is must-see art.

FAC Fabrica de Arte Cubano is a thriving, lively art gallery and nightclub. Mingle with tourists and locals alike and experience live art installations, music performances, and more.

Local galleries are scattered throughout the streets of Old Havana and have a varying degree of price and talent.

HUMANITARIAN / GIFTS FOR CUBANS

It is nice to bring gifts. Cubans have access to very little, and anything helps.

Casa owners are probably some of the more well-off families in Cuba. Often, the host families employ people to do the work in the house, and they typically get paid about ten dollars a month for working part-time in a private house. Bringing small gifts for these workers is very much appreciated.

- Toiletries/feminine products
- Clothing
- Colored pens/pencils/notepads
- White acrylic paint for artists
- Coloring books
- Balls (baseballs, soccer balls, etc.)

INTERNET

Internet in Cuba is unpredictable at best. Wi-Fi typically costs $4/hour, and although it is not guaranteed, there is usually a signal at Parque Central Hotel, and a few others.

http://www.hotelparquecentral-cuba.com/

OUTSIDE OF HAVANA

Viñales

Best known for its tobacco farms, languid lifestyle, and the distinctive limestone hills of Valle de Viñales.

Las Terrazes

A UNESCO biosphere reserve, a burgeoning activity center (with a canopy tour), and the site of the earliest coffee plantations in Cuba.

Spruce Up Your Spanish

English	Spanish	Pronunciation
Yes	Sí	see
No	No	noh
Yes, please	Sí, por favor	see por fah-bor
No, thank you	No, gracias	noh grah-thyas
Please	Por favor	por fah-bor
Thank you	Gracias	grah-thyas
You're welcome	De nada	deh nah-dah
Here is/are . . .	Aquí está/están . . .	ah-kee es-tah/es-tan
Hello	Hola	oh-lah
Good morning	Buenos días	bweh-nos dee-as
Good afternoon	Buenas tardes	bweh-nas tar-des
Goodbye	Adiós	ah-dyos
Good night	Buenas noches	bweh-nas noh-ches
How are you?	¿Cómo está?	koh-moh es-tah
Very well, thanks.	Muy bien, gracias.	mwee byen grah-thyas
Excuse me	Disculpe	dees-kool-peh
Do you speak English?	¿Habla usted inglés?	ah-blah oo-steth een-gles
Can you help me?	¿Me puede ayudar?	meh poo-eh-deh ah-yoo-dar
I don't understand.	No entiendo.	noh en-tyehn-doh
I don't know.	No lo sé.	noh loh seh

Hola

Liza Gershman is an award-winning photographer and writer, and seasoned world traveler. Passionate about food, people, and culture, Liza has had the opportunity to photograph in more than forty-five countries and forty-six US states during her career.

Liza teaches workshops, gives lectures, and writes articles on photography for Canon USA. She has worked as the Senior Digital Photographer for Williams-Sonoma, freelances for Restoration Hardware, is a Getty Image Contributor, and has photographed eleven cocktail and cookbooks for numerous publishers in the US.

In 2010, Liza was governor Jerry Brown's campaign photographer, and in 2014 she was the lead photographer for the Red Bull Youth America's Cup Team NZ2. Many of her additional clients have included celebrity chefs, wineries, beverage brands, and restaurants.

Published books include:

- Passage to China (Skyhorse Publishing, 2017)
- Drink Vermont: Flavors of The Green Mountain State (Skyhorse Publishing, 2017)
- The Good Cook's Book of Tomatoes (Skyhorse Publishing, 2015)
- The Good Cook's Book of Mustard (Skyhorse Publishing, 2015)
- The Good Cook's Book of Oil & Vinegar (Skyhorse Publishing, 2015)
- The Good Cook's Book of Salt & Pepper (Skyhorse Publishing, 2015)
- The Good Cook's Journal (Skyhorse Publishing, 2015)
- More Than Meatballs (Skyhorse Publishing, 2014)
- Be Fabulous at Any Age (LionsGate Corporation, 2013)
- San Francisco Entertains: The Junior League of San Francisco's Centennial Cookbook (Favorite Recipes Press, 2011)
- A Taste for Absinthe (Clarkson Potter, a division of Random House, 2010)

Publications include:

Maxim.com, SI.com, Outside Magazine, Huffington Post, Wine Spectator, NBC Bay Area, Chicago Sun Times, C Magazine, Daily Candy, SF Gate, San Francisco Chronicle, Seattle PI, Tasting Panel Magazine, Foodandwine.com, Fairfield County Look, Napa Valley Life, St. Helena Star, Eater SF, Beer Connoisseur, Wine X Magazine, Publisher's Weekly, Nightclub & Bar, Gig Salad, Tasting Table, MindFood (Australia and New Zealand), VSCO, and Food Arts Magazine, to name a few.

Clients include:

Canon USA, Williams-Sonoma, Restoration Hardware, Safeway, Jerry Brown for Governor, Red Bull Youth America's Cup Full Metal Jacket Racing Team, Airbnb, SandBox Studios, Grand Hyatt San Francisco, and more.

Index

Conversion Charts

METRIC AND IMPERIAL CONVERSIONS
(These conversions are rounded for convenience)

Ingredient	Cups/Table-spoons/Teaspoons	Ounces	Grams/Milliliters
Butter	1 cup = 16 table-spoons = 2 sticks	8 ounces	230 grams
Cheese, shredded	1 cup	4 ounces	110 grams
Cream cheese	1 tablespoon	0.5 ounce	14.5 grams
Cornstarch	1 tablespoon	0.3 ounce	8 grams
Flour, all-purpose	1 cup/1 tablespoon	4.5 ounces/0.3 ounce	125 grams/8 grams
Flour, whole wheat	1 cup	4 ounces	120 grams
Fruit, dried	1 cup	4 ounces	120 grams
Fruits or veggies, chopped	1 cup	5 to 7 ounces	145 to 200 grams
Fruits or veggies, puréed	1 cup	8.5 ounces	245 grams
Honey, maple syrup, or corn syrup	1 tablespoon	.75 ounce	20 grams
Liquids: cream, milk, water, or juice	1 cup	8 fluid ounces	240 milliliters
Oats	1 cup	5.5 ounces	150 grams
Salt	1 teaspoon	0.2 ounce	6 grams
Spices: cinnamon, cloves, ginger, or nutmeg (ground)	1 teaspoon	0.2 ounce	5 milliliters
Sugar, brown, firmly packed	1 cup	7 ounces	200 grams
Sugar, white	1 cup/1 tablespoon	7 ounces/0.5 ounce	200 grams/12.5 grams
Vanilla extract	1 teaspoon	0.2 ounce	4 grams

OVEN TEMPERATURES

Fahrenheit	Celsius	Gas Mark
225°	110°	$\frac{1}{4}$
250°	120°	$\frac{1}{2}$
275°	140°	1
300°	150°	2
325°	160°	3
350°	180°	4
375°	190°	5
400°	200°	6
425°	220°	7
450°	230°	8